Dull stocks, Hot Options!

Chiu-ying Wong, CFA

First edition : April 2012
Second edition : August 2012
Third edition : February 2012
Fourth edition : March 2013

ISBN-10: 1475001711
ISBN-13: 978-1475001716
Published by www.dullbooks.com
Read more at www.ProfitFromOptions.com

CONTENTS

1   INTRODUCTION

Why should we trade options?

Since you are browsing or have already bought this book, you'd probably have some ideas of the benefits of trading options, so let me just summarize the main ones briefly below.

Stock investing used to be easy. Buy good stocks and hold them forever. Since the end of the twentieth century, the financial market became more complicated. More financial products were developed and introduced to retail investors. The global economic landscape also became more intertwined. These all resulted in more rapid change in fortunes of companies as well as the shifting of importance of factors that impact stock prices.

Some stock investors may think that spending more time in improving stock investing skills would be sufficient to increase the profitability of their stock investments. However, experienced stock investors also know that there are periods of time and sets of circumstances when stock fundamentals matter little, and market sentiments dominate the stage. Just look at 2011.

The world economy was in a recovery in 2009 and 2010. In the first half of 2011, on the third year of the recovery from the 2008 financial crisis, the US stock market ran out of steam. The money printing activities of the US Federal Reserve, under the names of Quantitative Easing 1 (QE1) and Quantitative Easing 2 (QE2), had created a large volume of money (liquidity) in the financial market, allowing banks and companies to borrow cheap and improve earnings. But the progress of improvement had slowed down by 2011. Unemployment did not come down much. There was also a debt crisis in the Euro zone, with bad news coming from Greece, Spain, and Portugal on a regular basis. These two forces counteracted each other, producing a directionless market since May 2011.

The second half of 2011, on the other hand, provides an example of a volatile market affected by the same macro factors. While the worsened negative news from Europe drove the stock markets down in general, hopes and better news created spikes from time to time. The S&P500 became more volatile in the second half of 2011. After the sharp drop in August 2011, S&P500 moved from week to week in a jerky manner that was not seen in the early part of 2011.

If you had owned shares of large companies listed in the USA like those belonging to the S&P500 index, your returns would probably be similar to that of the stock SPY, an exchange traded fund that aims to duplicate the performance of the S&P500. As can be seen from the chart of SPY below, you would have had to endure the dull performance in the first half of 2011, and then suffered the stomach-churning volatility in the third quarter of the year, to find in December 2011 that you ended up where you started.

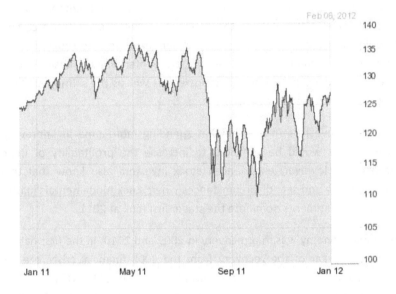

Source: Yahoo Finance

If you had invested outside of the list of big cap stocks, the swings would most likely to have been even bigger. For individual stocks, in addition to the general market conditions, investors have to watch out also for events that can impact stock price significantly, such as: before earnings announcement, product announcement, changes in relevant regulatory provisions. Most investors are not able to time such swings successfully.

While a high volatility period may not last long, it could be psychologically stressful and cause some investors to make trading mistakes. For equity investors, the only benefit of a volatile period is if one can find the bottom and buy stocks at good price before it recovers. But that is not an easy task. There are option trading strategies that allow equity investors to make money during times of high volatility, regardless of where the stock price ends.

To have success in investing in stocks, an investor needs to identify the time when the price of a stock is going to go up. He or she will not be able to make money when the investor knows that the stock price will stay within a particular range in a specific timeframe. We can use option strategies to make profit in such situations.

Options can also allow investors to gain the same stock exposure with much less capital, or bet on the fall of a stock price with limited downside risk.

In sum, option strategies give you the tools to make money in more situations than what is possible in stock trading. In an era where those who have capital and technology can use computers to scrape off even the thinnest profit available from stock trading before others can see it, retail investors need every edge we can get. But there is no free lunch. Only those who are prepared to take the time to learn how options work can use them profitably.

What this book can do for you

This book will teach you how to think through an option trade. It will arm you with an understanding of the mechanics of options trading so that you can use the knowledge to leverage your stock investing expertise. It is not an idiot's guide to get rich quick. You will need to analyze your stock and make assessment about its future. Then you can use the knowledge gained from this book to select the optimal options strategy to achieve your objective. Many option books will give you a menu of tens of different option strategies, with only a basic explanation of what each one is about, and tell you to choose an option strategy based on the payoff graph only. I will say this now and again, trading options on the basis of payoff graphs alone is a sure way to lose money.

You will learn about the most relevant characteristics of an option, so that you can use the right option in the correct way.

You will learn to focus on the important points in selecting an option strategy to best take advantage of a particular situation.

You will learn to assess alternatives when the market goes against your trade. This would help you remain calm and avoid costly mistakes that could be made if you were in a panic.

This book will also give some suggestions on ways to treat option positions in a portfolio management setting. Stock options should not be viewed in isolation. They are most successful when seen as a part of your stock investing activities, because they depend on your views on stock price movements, and enhance the returns potentials from such views. You can also choose a particular option strategy so as to modify the risk return profile of your stock portfolio, and as a result, the performance of your total asset portfolio.

It will also touch on the important issues of the trader's psychology and mental limits, since we are human and not machines.

Risk and reward

What we get when a trade goes our way is the reward. When a trade turns sour, the worst loss is the risk, right? That would be only part of our consideration of risk and reward in evaluating a potential trade. Apart from the size of the gain or loss, we should also be concerned about the chances of an event, such as the maximum gain or maximum loss, happening. A highly profitable trade may not be very desirable if the chances of it actually happening is very low. Conversely, trades that only entail the loss of a small amount are not low risk if the likelihood of that loss is very high.

For each basic option strategy covered in this book, there will be a summary box providing the maximum gain and loss possible according to the payoff equations. Occasionally, I will also give my views on factors that could affect the chances of these two events in the summary box. However, each stock has its own price dynamics, and complex option positions add further to the difficulty in predicting the probability of events. In addition, during the life of an option, its price can differ from the value indicated by the payoff equation, as you will learn from the next chapters of this books. Use the summary box as a memory aid, but never as a trade recommendation. Do not be seduced by the size of the maximum gain or be deterred by the maximum loss without giving due consideration to the likelihood of either event.

We should also note that institutional stock investors use a different meaning for the word "risk" from option traders. To the stock investors, risk means deviation from the mean return. If two stocks each has a daily return of 0.8% on average over one year, the stock that had experienced returns that were very high and very low compared to this mean is regarded as more risky than the other whose returns stayed around the mean all the time. While some stock investors do not like this kind of fluctuation in returns (and thus price), option traders see opportunities in volatility. We will explain how this can be the case in the next chapter. The point that I wish to make here is that when we hear about the term 'risk', it could mean different things to stock investors and option traders.

2 A QUICK PEEK INTO THE WORLD OF OPTIONS

Options in a nutshell

While the rest of the book will cover a lot of details about options, it would be useful to give you an outline of this financial product first, so that you can maintain a frame of reference when more information is added later.

A stock option is a contract which gives the buyer (also called the holder) of the option the **right** to buy (or sell) the underlying stock at a pre-agreed price (called the strike price or exercise price) on or before a specific date (called the expiration date). After the expiration date, the contract no longer exists. In exchange for such a right, the buyer has to pay a price (called option premium) at the start of the contract. For options traded in an options exchange that is open to the public (i.e. exchanged listed options), the other legal party of the contract (the counterparty) is either an options exchange or an options clearing body like the Options Clearing Corporation (OCC) in the USA. For each contract that the counterparty (e.g. a clearing body) enters into with an option buyer, the counterparty will also enter into a matching contract with someone who is willing to sell the option. The role of the exchange or clearing body is to ensure that promises made in the contract by the parties to it are delivered.

The seller (also called writer) of the option has an **obligation** to sell (or buy) the underlying stock at the strike price at the request of the other contract party. As compensation for taking up the obligation, the option seller (or writer) gets to receive the option premium.

Options in which the buyer agrees to buy the stocks underlying the option contracts are called **call options**. Options in which the buyer agrees to sell the stocks underlying the option contracts are called **put options**.

There are two main *styles* of options: American and European. These two styles differ by the existence of a right by the option buyer to 'exercise' the options contract before the agreed expiration date. The option seller has to deliver what is promised in the options contract when the contract is exercised. When a call option buyer exercises the stock option, it means he/she wants to pay the agreed price to gain possession of the shares underlying the stock option. The seller can do nothing but oblige and deliver the shares to the counterparty of the option contract. When a put option buyer exercises the stock option, the seller will have to buy shares from the counterparty at the agreed (strike) price. American style options can be exercised any time during the life of the option, while European style options can be exercised only on expiration. Almost all options listed in US options exchanges are American style.

This book primarily covers American style options, although many of the concepts are applicable to European style options also. Some brokers may allow European options to be traded (i.e. bought and sold) before expiration, but the valuation would be different from American style options due to the exercise feature.

The main points to take home here are:

A.   Options are financial products with limited shelf life; and
B.   The relationship between option buyers and option sellers is similar to that between an insurance policy holder and the insurance company. The buyers pay a premium so that they will receive a larger sum of money if some event occurs on or before the contract expires.

The options market

Stock options are traded on exchanges in almost all major financial centers around the world. An investor can open an account with one of those online brokers who offer stock and options trading services for international markets, and trade options listed in exchanges in USA, Canada, Germany, United Kingdom, Australia, Japan and Hong Kong.

The USA has the largest options market in the world. It has nine options exchanges, including CBOE Holdings Inc., Nasdaq OMX Group's PHLX and NOM, International Securities Exchange, NYSE's Amex and Arca. Trading volume for U.S.-listed equity options in 2011 totaled 4.22 billion contracts, a 17.02 percent increase from the previous peak of 3.6 billion contracts bought and sold in 2010. Deutsche Boerse AG, which owns ISE, and NYSE Euronext, which owns Amex and Arca, were merged in late 2011, and together they handled 40.3 per cent of all options trade in July 2011. CBOE, which also owns the electronic C2 market, handled 26.2 per cent, while Nasdaq handled 25.9 per cent.

For those who are considering investing either in US options market or options markets in other countries, I would recommend that you trade the US options market because of its depth and breadth. The US options market is more liquid than other markets and market information is more readily available. The cost of transaction is also the lowest. Options that have a low volume of transactions tend to have wide bid/ask spread, and this becomes a cost (e.g. if you want to sell an option even immediately after you bought it, the market only offers you a price that is much lower than the price you paid). If you are residing in a country outside US, it should not be difficult for you to find companies with international exposure listed in the US stock and options markets. In almost all corners of the world, people are aware of companies like Coca Cola, Proctor and Gamble, Microsoft and so on. Many large corporations with overseas headquarters are also listed on US stock market either directly or in the form of American Depository Receipts (ADRs), and many of them have options listed in the US options market also. Examples are Baidu Inc. (BIDU) from China, Credit Suisse (CS) from Switzerland, ICICI Bank (IBN) from India and so on. You should not have much problem in building up a knowledge base of these companies for stock and options trading. The US stock and options markets are also very accessible to foreigners. Nowadays, there are quite a number of brokers, based in USA or abroad, that allow foreigners to trade US listed stocks and stock options.

What it takes to trade options
I will be honest. Options trading is not for everyone. If someone tells you that trading option is simple, that you can master it from reading one book or attending one training course, or by subscribing to a newsletter that can tell you where to place your bets, do not believe that person.

Options trading require a great respect for downside risk. An option can involve leverage (we will explain leverage a bit more later), thus your gain and loss can be substantial as measured against the money that you put in. Therefore, you must know your capacity and tolerance for downside risk, and are willing to take actions to manage it. For example, when a stock price goes down by 3%, the value of some options could go down by 20% or more. You would need to accept a higher level of volatility when you trade options than what you would normally experience in trading stocks.

Second, just like in stock trading, investors will have to be familiar with the factors that affect the price of an option. These factors, however, are in addition to factors that influence stock prices, because they are related to the nature of this financial product called options. Quite often an investor has to take into account more than one factor impacting the option price at any one time. While not many stocks will lose all of their value even over a long period of time, in options trading, ignoring the other factors and focusing only on the price of the underlying could bring ruin very fast. Thus investors must be willing to handle an additional set of factors when trading options of stocks.

Third, you need to have patience when trading options. This may sound counterintuitive at first, since I have talked so much about how rapid option value can change over a short period of time. You may get the impression that option trading is suitable for people with itchy fingers who are ready to pull the trigger on a few seconds' notice. That is only partly true. An option trader should also be like a fisherman who would wait patiently most of the time and act quickly only when certain conditions come into place. Not that you don't need patience in trading stocks, but it matters more in options. If you buy a stock too early, you may give up 10 or 20% of gain, the same mistake in options could cause you substantial loss.

Four, you need to have a list of stocks that you are familiar with, so that you can decide quickly whether there is trading opportunities when special events happen to them. Many experienced options traders only trade options of a few stocks, using different strategies to produce profits under various stock price scenarios.

What you do not need to trade options

Even though trading options require you to pay attention to several parameters at the same time, you do not need to have a PhD in mathematics. You just need to remember the basic characteristics of several important parameters, be discipline about when to trade, and be diligent enough to implement risk management measures.

Leverage or not

Investopedia.com defines leverage as "the use of various financial instruments or borrowed capital, such as margin, to increase the potential return of an investment". In other words, to obtain the effect of magnified return, you can use either borrowed money or financial instruments like options. When you use options to get leverage, some options would involve borrowed money and some would not. Those that involve borrowed money (like selling options) are considered more dangerous than those that do not involve borrowed money, as you will be taking a chance of losing more money than what you put on the table. Those that do not involve borrowed money (like buying options), on the other hand, reduce the chance that you could make a profit, as you have to pay a fee (premium) to enter into a trade. There is no free lunch.

Stock options vs stock warrants vs binary options

Some securities exchanges offer stock warrants for trading. While stock warrants are also financial instruments that derive their value from underlying stocks, they are very different from stock options. The major difference between the two is in the supply side of the instruments. For options, investors can sell options without owning the options first, i.e. sell to open a position. For warrants, only the issuer can increase the supply of warrants in the market. The latter situation creates an additional and crucial factor to the pricing of the warrants. For example, when there is good news about a stock, demand for its call options and warrants is likely to go up. While this could induce more people to sell options and thus moderate the rise in the value of option premium, the warrant issuer can choose to increase the supply of warrants only when the warrant price has gone up to unjustifiable height, and then buy them back when the price has deflated. I have no proof to show that warrant issuers actually do that, but it is a fact that warrant supply is controlled by the issuer only. At the very least, due to this difference, many strategies that are available to option traders are not available to warrant investors.

Binary options are being offered by a large number of small companies that operate from all corners of the world. Do not be fooled by the presence of the word 'options' in their name. These trades are nothing like ordinary options traded on the options exchanges. The only thing that they have in common with ordinary stock options is that their payout is based on the stock price on expiration of the contract. The key word in the name is 'binary', which means the payout is either 0 or 100% of the payout amount agreed at the start of the contract between the seller (which is usually the company offering the 'trading platform') and the buyer, usually a member of the public. The trade is only cash settled, and no physical delivery of the underlying stock is ever involved. Even CBOE, the Chicago Board Options Exchange, is getting in the act, although their version of binary options, with multiple strike prices and longer expiration and premiums related to the probability of the options being in the money, is more like ordinary options than those offered by the small companies which have no other securities related business.

The expiration time is very short, from a few minutes to a few hours, or, in the case of CBOE, one month, and the payout can be regarded more like the payout from a roulette table in a casino than anything else. For example, you can enter into a contract that bets that, in two hours, the price of a stock will be higher than the current stock price. If you bet right, you will get a payout of one hundred dollars per contract in the case of CBOE, while the premium per contract is between one to one hundred dollars. If you bet wrong, you do not get anything back. If you bet odd or even numbers on a roulette table, you would usually get 100% payout if your bet is correct. Stock price movement in a very short period of time is more likely to be a random walk than following any rule. But some people who think they can read chart well may think they have an edge. I do not belong to that camp, and I think a lot of people are in my camp.

3   OPTION ESSENTIALS

Basic contract types

There are two types of options contract that an investor can trade: call options and put options. But because you can either buy or sell each type of options, there are actually four types of trade that you can initiate. To distinguish the option buyer's (holder's) position from the option seller's (writer's) position, we will refer to the owning of an option as a **long** position, e.g. a long call position means that we are looking from the option buyer's angle. We will refer to the option seller's position as a **short** option position, e.g. a short call position means that we are looking from the option seller's angle. Option trading is a zero sum game. The option buyer's gain will be the option seller's loss, and vice versa. Therefore, when we say that a long call option has a positive value, it implies that a corresponding short call option will have a negative value of the same size.

i.   Call options

The buyer of a call option pays a fee to get a chance to make a profit when the price of a stock exceeds a certain value (strike price) on or before a preset date (expiration date). In other words, the buyer of a call option hopes to profit when the price of a stock rises.

The seller (also referred as the writer) of a call option receives a fee to take the risk of having to sell the shares of a stock underlying an option at the strike price if the market price of the stock exceeds the strike price on or before the expiration date. The seller of a call option believes that the stock price is unlikely to rise above the strike price during the life of the option.

ii.   Put options

The buyer of a put option pays a fee to get a chance to make a profit when the price of a stock is less than a certain value on a preset date. In general, the buyer of a put option thinks that the price of a stock will fall.

The seller of a put option receives the fee paid by the option buyer, and takes the risk of having to buy the shares of the stock underlying the option at the strike price if the market price of the stock falls below the strike price on or before the option expires. The seller of a put option believes that the stock price is unlikely to fall below the strike price during the life of the option.

Common features

As mentioned, each option has a strike price, and an expiration date. The strike price is a predetermined price that will be compared against the price of the stock for calculating whether the option has any value. After the expiration date, an option will have no value and will cease to exist.

Therefore, if an investor wants to trade options on a stock, he/she will have to select the strike price and expiration date of the option, and also specify at what price he is willing to buy/sell the option.

From the above brief description of the two option types, trading options would seem straightforward: we will buy a call option if we have a bullish opinion about a stock, and buy a put option if we have a bearish opinion. Unfortunately, reality is more complicated than we would like it to be. There are more factors to consider in trading options than we would like to know. We will go into some of the more important ones later. I will first show you the payoff and profit/loss graphs of the two types of options at expiration.

1. Payoff

The call option payoff is what a call option buyer can get according to the options contract if he/she exercises the option or holds the option to expiration. The payoff calculation assumes that, in exercising the option or when the option expires, the investor pays the agreed (strike) price for the shares underlying the option, and then sells the shares he/she receives immediately at market price. The difference between the market price and the strike is the payoff. What the buyer can get is what the seller can lose.

The payoff equation for a call option is:

Call option payoff = max((stock price − strike price), 0)

In plain English, the equation says that the payoff is either the value of stock price minus strike price, or zero, whichever is higher.

It can be seen easily from the equation that, first, there is no payoff if the stock price is less than the strike price. Second, payoff increases in lock step with the stock price once the stock price exceeds the strike price. For a call option with strike at $30, for example, the payoff would be $5 if the stock price is $35 when the option is exercised. If the stock price rises further to $38, payoff will increase to $8 ($38-$30). At any price equal to or below $30, the payoff would be zero.

The put option payoff is what a put option buyer can get according to the options contract if he/she exercises the option or holds the option to expiration. It assumes that the option buyer sells the shares underlying the option at the strike price, and then buys them back immediately in the open market.

Put option payoff = max((strike price – stock price), 0)

There is no payoff if the stock price is equal to or greater than the strike price. For a put option with strike at $30, the payoff would be $4 if the stock price is $26 when the option is exercised. At any price equal to or above $30, the payoff would be zero.

Payoff is NOT the price that you will get when you trade an option before it expires. The latter, known as the value of an option, is determined by a number of factors in addition to the prevailing stock price, and is the heart of option trading. For example, when the payoff of an option is zero, as long as the option is not near expiration, the option can still have a positive value.

The most common divergence between payoff and the value of an option occurs with the change in current stock price. While payoff of a call option increases by the same size as the increase in the underlying stock price, for example, the value of that option can go up by a very different amount, and in some instances, can even go the opposite direction. A large part of this book is used to explain these instances. Upon expiration, though, payoff and market value of an option will converge.

If an option buyer exercises the option before it expires, he/she will forego the value of the option, which he/she could have received if the option is sold instead of exercised. Since option value before expiration is usually higher than the payoff, investors do not exercise options before expiration in most cases. This is the reason why the value of an option is the more important consideration than payoff for an option investor in most circumstances, unless the investor intends to hold the option until it expires.

A **payoff graph** is a graph that shows the payoff of an option at various prices of the underlying stock. Since payoff and the value of an option are the same at expiration, a payoff graph can be seen as a graph showing the value of an option at expiration. A payoff graph can be drawn from either the angle of a buyer, or that of a seller.

A **profit/loss graph** is the payoff graph plus (or minus) the option premium received (or paid) at the beginning of an option trade. Thus, the graph shows how well you would do with a trade taking into account other income and expenditure at different stock prices upon option expiration or if it is exercised. As in the case of the payoff graph, the profit/loss graph does not take into account the value of the option if the option is to be exercised before its expiration. For simplicity purpose, we assume in these graphs that commissions and other trading costs are negligible, but by all means you should include them in your own profit/loss calculation.

For a long call option position, the payoff and profit/loss graphs will look something like those below:

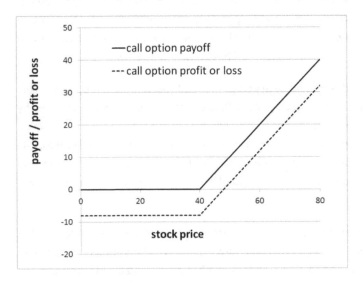

The above diagram contains (i) payoff and (ii) profit/loss graphs for a call option that was bought for a call premium of $8 and with a strike price of $40. The long call position has a positive payoff when the stock price is above the strike price. However, it will only become profitable when the stock price is above the strike price plus the option premium, i.e. $40 + $8 = $48.

For a call option seller, the graphs will be the vertically opposite of the buyer's graphs. An option seller will never have a positive payoff, but he/she will receive a profit, albeit limited to a maximum of the premium received, if the stock price does not go above the strike price plus the premium, which is $48.

You may recall that the put option payoff equation is as follows:

$$\text{payoff} = \max((\text{strike price} - \text{stock price at option expiration}), 0)$$

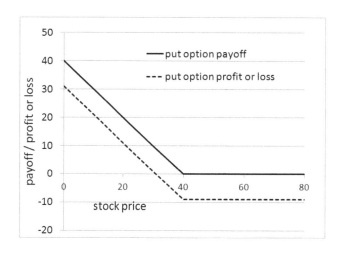

The above diagram contains the payoff and profit/loss graphs for a long put option position with a strike price of $40 and premium of $9. The option buyer will have a positive payoff if the stock price goes below the strike price. The option position will only be profitable, however, if the stock price is below the strike price minus the option premium, i.e. below $40 - $9 = $31.

For a seller of a put option, the graphs will look like these:

The short put option position does not have positive payoff at any stock price. It has a negative payoff when the stock price is below the strike price. It has a profit only when the stock price is above the strike price minus the option premium, i.e. $40 - $9 = $31.

To recap, payoff graphs for each pair of options buyer and seller look like the vertical mirror image of each other. On either the left or right hand side of the graph, it is a flat line. If the stock price falls within the range covered by the flat line, then the option buyer has zero payoff. At the strike price, the graph starts to become a slope. If the stock price falls within the slope portion on expiration of the option contract, then the option buyer will have a positive payoff while the seller will experience negative payoff of the same magnitude.

Similarly, the profit or loss graph for an options buyer and its seller is the vertical mirror image of each other. However, profit for an option buyer starts to be positive only after the full cost of the option premium is covered. An option seller will start to incur losses if the value of the payoff to the option buyer exceeds the option premium. In other words, the option premium provides a cushion for the option seller.

2. Moneyness of options

There are three terms to describe the different payoff states of an option. They are phrased from the viewpoint of an option buyer.

Out of money - When, using the option payoff formula, the long option position does not have a positive payoff, we will say that the option is Out Of Money (OTM). For call options, this is when the stock price is less than the strike price. For put options, this is when the stock price exceeds the strike price. When an option is OTM for an option buyer, the corresponding option seller should be in a good mood, since the position is in the seller's favor. The option buyer would have no incentive to exercise the option, so the seller is likely to be able to keep all the option premium. For a call option with strike at $40, for example, it is OTM when the stock price is less than $40. For a put option with the same strike price, it is OTM when the stock price exceeds $40.

At the money - When the stock price equals the strike price, the option is at the money (ATM). If an option is ATM, it will not likely be exercised since the option does not have any payoff. ATM is a very delicate state of an option, as a small movement of any of the several parameters that affect an option's value will change its state, from OTM to In-The-Money (ITM) or vice versa. An option buyer would like to see an option move from ATM to ITM, rather than from ATM to OTM.

In the money - When, using the option payoff formula, the option has a positive payoff, we will say that the option is In The Money (ITM). For call options, this is when the stock price is above the strike price. For put options, this is when the stock price is below the strike price.

Because option value under different states (ITM, ATM or OTM) is impacted differently by external factors, these three terms are useful for you to distinguish between the strategies that you would like to employ in a particular situation. For example, if you buy a deep ITM call option, you would be most likely looking for a gradual move (as opposed to a rapid, highly volatile move) in stock price and a lock step rise in option value (a high delta play, to be explained in the next chapter). You may also not mind buying additional shares of the stock at the strike price, because the option would be highly likely to be ITM on expiration and exercised automatically. If you buy an OTM call option, then you are likely to be looking for a rapid rise in stock price in the near future (a volatility play), and stand ready to sell the option to close after the expected event have happened (or not) and before it expires. You are unlikely to be interested in owing additional shares of that stock.

When stock price goes up (or down), will you be richer or poorer?

We have mentioned that the payoff of a long option position is proportion to the difference between the strike price and the spot price of the stock. Thus, the outcome of your option trade is easy to see at option expiration.

However, most options are not held to expiration, because there are many opportunities for making a profit during the course of the life of an option, or sometimes because losses could be reduced by closing an option position early.

Many option positions are closed before they expire even when the payoff is unfavorable. To explain why investors would do that, we need to consider, before option expiration, the probability of the stock price reaching the strike price on expiration. The change in stock price is an important factor influencing that probability, but there are other factors at work. If the stock price is at the strike price near the option expiration, it is of course very likely, but still not certain, that the stock price will remain equal to the strike price on expiration. If there is a lot of time before the option expires, then the move of the stock price closer to the strike price will not have much predictive power regarding option value on expiration. We will examine these important factors later.

From the profit or loss graphs, you can see that whether you will come out richer or poorer from an option trade depends, of course, also on how much you paid at the start of the option contract if you are an option buyer, or how much you received if you are an option seller, versus how much you receive or pay when you close your options position. Therefore, we need to understand how the current option price came about *before* opening a position either to buy or sell an option, so that we can benefit from the eventual path taken by the option value before reaching expiration.

3. Time Value of an option

The options equations give the value of an option when it is exercised or upon expiration. This payoff value is also called the **intrinsic value** of the option. For example, for a long call option with a strike price of $10, if the current stock price is $13, then the intrinsic value of that option would be $3. Before an option expires, an investor who has bought an option from an exchange can sell it back on the exchange at the prevailing price of the option (its market price), and that would close the option position; similarly, an investor who has sold an option can buy it back on the exchange at the market price and exit the position. The difference between the market value of an option and the intrinsic value is called the time value of an option. Using the same example, if that call option is selling for $4.30 in the open market, then $1.30 would be the time value.

What is the time value of a call option with a strike price of $10 and an option price of $0.80 when the current stock price is $9.50? The time value would be $0.80, as an out-of-money (OTM) option does not have any intrinsic value, and the option value is all time value, reflecting, in some people's view, the value that the market places on the possibility that the option can get back to be in-the-money (ITM) in the remaining time before expiration. As a quick review, can you work out the intrinsic value of the option in the same example, assuming it is a put option instead?

As long as there is time left in the options contract, the options value can still be affected by factors not included in the options payoff equation. The most important of these factors will be explained in the next chapter.

Other options trading technicalities

Contract size

The standard option contract size is 100 shares of the underlying stock. For example, if the price of an option of stock XYZ is quoted as $1.20, it means that the buyer will have to pay $1.20 times 100 to purchase one option contract. The payoff from that contract will be 100 times the value indicated by the payoff equation. If the buyer (who is now a 'holder') of a call option wants to exercise the option, he/she will have to pay the strike price times 100 and get possession of 100 shares of stock XYZ. If it is a put option, the buyer who wants to exercise the option will receive an amount that equals to the strike price times 100 and have to deliver 100 shares of stock XYZ.

Option exercise rules

An option can be 'exercised' only by the option holder. That means, for a call option holder, you can exercise your right to buy the underlying stocks at the strike price, and for a put option holder, you can sell the underlying stocks at the strike price. For the call options holder, you will need to have sufficient money or credit line to pay for the stocks. For put options holder, you will need to have the underlying stocks to deliver to the put option seller.

If you want to exercise an option before expiration, you should find out beforehand the procedures of your broker, as different brokers have different requirements. Usually, it involves giving a notice a few hours before the market closes for the day (the broker's cutoff time). While theoretically, options can be exercised even when they are not in-the-money (ITM), not many people would do so because it is not profitable to do that most of the time.

If you hold options that are ITM on expiration, it depends on your broker's procedures on whether the options will be exercised automatically. Some brokers, who choose to follow the rules laid down by the option exchanges, will automatically exercise your call option if it is in-the-money by $0.1 or more on expiration. If your call option is ITM on expiration and you do not have sufficient cash to pay for the purchase of the underlying stocks, your broker may lend you money and subject you to interest charges. If your put option is automatically exercised and you do not have the underlying stocks to deliver, your broker will likely borrow the stocks for you, and after delivery, you will have a short stock position. Alternatively, you can give specific instruction not to exercise the option even on expiration, if allowed by your broker.

Contract expiration dates

All options have limited life span. The last day that an option exists is called the expiration date. Most of the stock options listed in USA exchanges expire on the third Saturday of the expiration month. Recently, weekly expiring options have been introduced, but they are mainly the domain of professional traders. Subject to your broker's specific requirement, option holders who want to exercise their option must submit their exercise notices to their brokers the latest on the Friday before that Saturday, unless the options belong to the auto-exercise type, in which case no notice is necessary. If that Friday happens to be a public holiday, then the option exercise notice will have to be submitted on the Thursday before instead. For historical reasons, US traded options for a particular stock have at least four expiration months in a year, and each expiration month falls within one of the three common expiration cycles:

January cycle (JAJO) – January, April, July, and October;

February cycle (FMAN) – February, May, August and November;

March cycle (MJSD) – March, June, September and December;

In addition to these four expiration months, options are also available for the current and the following months.

Options assignment rules

If you sell stock options, you are obliged to meet the demand of the option holders to buy the underlying shares (for call options) or sell the underlying shares (for put options) at the strike price when he/she chooses to exercise the option before expiration, or when his/her option is automatically exercised on expiration. If you trade index options on stock index, on the other hand, you do not need to deliver the actual stocks, but only the obligation in cash, i.e. the contract is said to be cash settled.

Since there are usually more options sellers than option holders that want/are required to exercise their options, when it receives an exercise notice, the US Options Clearing Corporation (OCC) will randomly assign option sellers to fulfill the exercise demand from option holders. If you are the seller of an ITM option and got 'assigned' to fulfill the option obligation, then you have to deliver whatever is due. For a call option seller, that means selling the underlying shares at the strike price. For a put option seller, that means buying the underlying shares at the strike price even though the market price of the shares is lower. The equivalent amount of cash will be deducted from your brokerage account.

Strike prices

Strike price is a reference price in an option contract at which the option holder has the right to buy (for a call option) or to sell (for a put option) the underlying shares of a stock. Strike price is also called exercise price.

Strike prices for each options series (i.e. all the available options for the same underlying stock with the same expiration date) are established by the respective options exchanges. They follow some conventions, such as for strike prices below $25, the option strike prices often have a $2.50 interval, while for options with strike prices above $25, the strike price interval is usually $5, but options exchanges can also introduce options at strike prices that take into account changes in the stock price or in response to market demand or unusual market conditions.

In 2003, the Securities and Exchanges Commission in US allowed options exchanges to introduce options with $1 strike price intervals for a limited number of stocks. According to the exchanges, the program was a major success. Trading volume and liquidity were much higher than before. Should that be a surprise? I do not think so. For small value stocks, an interval of $2.50 is simply too big. If a stock has a price of $5, the closest options would be available at $2.50, $5.0 and $7.50 only. Would you trade if you think that the stock price will be at $3.50 in a specific timeframe? You would either have to buy options that are likely to become deep ITM ($2.50) or far OTM ($5.00), paying more than you would for closer priced options in the former case, or bear a reduced chance of success in the latter. If the authorities want to promote options trading, smaller price intervals would be a good way to go.

Commission

Some brokers charge commission on per trade basis, others charge on per contract basis, and some others charge a variable commission based on the number of contracts. For example, Charles Schwab charges $8.95 per online trade, plus $0.75 per contract, OptionsHouse charges $5 for a trade of up to five contracts, plus $1 per additional contract, while Interactivebrokers charges $0.25 to $0.75 per contract, with a minimum of $1 per trade.

What impact does different commission structures have on your trading decisions? Commission structures that are per contract based are biased against options that have low value. For example, in August 2011, many options of Bank of America stock (stock price at around $7) have premium (or option price) of below $1. This means that each contract has value of less than $100. It is obvious that if you only trade one contract, the commission could be a high percentage of the total option premium value. Suppose you want to trade 100 contracts. Your commission would be lower on average, but could still be more than 1% of the total premium value (e.g. $75 of commission for premium value of $7000).

If you trade 10 contracts of Baidu's (BIDU) options, the stock price of which traded in the range of $94 to $165 in 2011, and each option has premium of $7, the total premium value would be the same at $7,000, while the commission is between $7.50 and $16, a big percentage difference, though small in amount.

As you can see, commission can be a very small part of the cost of options trading, if you do not trade low value options. Thus, you should consider other factors when choosing a broker, the main one being financial soundness of the company, followed by trade execution, trading platforms (since most people will use internet to trade) and trade volume. For US brokerage houses, you can refer to Barron's Annual Survey of Online Brokerages for guide.

Margins

Margin is the amount of cash that has to be set aside when you sell an option to meet obligations in case the trade goes against your bet. This means that you do not have to set aside the full amount of maximum potential loss for some trades if your broker allows margins for those trades. For example, if you sell a call option, you will lose money if stock price is above the strike price on expiration. The loss in theory could be unlimited, since the price of any stock could go up to any value. Thus, some brokers will not allow you to sell call options unless you own the corresponding number of shares of the underlying stock (such trades are called covered short call options). That way, you can always meet the options obligation no matter what price the underlying stock rises to, because the loss in the option trade can be made up for by the gain in the shares of the underlying stock.

Those brokers that allow you to sell a call option without ownership of the underlying stock (naked call option) have their own ways of calculating the margin you need to start the trade (initial margin) or to keep the trade alive (maintenance margin). Some do not bother to explain the margin very much in their website, but I believe most of them follow the recommendations of Chicago Board Options Exchange. For naked short call option, the recommended margin requirement is (take a deep breath first):

"100% of option proceeds plus 20% of underlying security value less out-of-the-money amount, if any, to a minimum for calls of option proceeds plus 10% of the underlying security value." (for short put, replace last sentence with:"..a minimum for puts of option proceeds plus 10% of the put's exercise price.")

What on earth does that mean? It means to work out the exact margin requirement, you would need to compute two values first, and then take the one that is higher. CBOE provided some examples, which can illustrate how the formulae work. (CBOE has adopted metric unit for option prices for many years, but as of end 2011, it has not updated the margin manual.) More information can be found in their website:

http://www.cboe.com/micro/margin/introduction.aspx

I reproduce below some of the examples that they use in the box below for the basic option strategies.

Box 1   Margin examples

OTM short call position
Short 1 Feb 30 call at 1/16 *(=0.0625)*
Underlying security at 17-3/8 *(=17.375)*

Margin Calculation: 100 x .0625 = $ 6.25	*(A=100% of option proceeds)*
20% x 100 x 17.375 = 347.50	*(B=20% of the underlying security value)*
(30 - 17.375) x 100 = (1,262.50)	*(C=out-of-money amount)*
Sum = $ (908.75)	*(D=A+B+C)*
Therefore, minimum applies:	
100 x .0625 = $ 6.25	*(A)*
10% x 100 x 17.375 = 173.75	*(E=10% of the underlying security value)*
Sum = $180.00	*(F=A+E)*

Margin Requirement: $180.00
SMA Debit or Margin Call: $180.00 - $6.25 = $173.75
Explanation: The margin requirement is 100% of the option proceeds plus 20% of the underlying security value less out-of-the-money amount, if any, to a minimum for calls of 100% of the option proceeds plus 10% of the underlying security value. The minimum applies in this example because the resulting margin requirement is greater than that of the basic formula. The sale proceeds may be applied to the **initial** margin requirement.

(Note: words and numbers in italics within brackets are added by me to help reading. The rest is taken from the CBOE margin manual.)

ITM short call position
Short 1 Nov 120 call at 8-3/8
Underlying security at 128-1/2

> *Margin Calculation:* 100 x 8.375 = $ 837.50
> 20% x 100 x 128.50 = 2,570.00
> Sum=$3,407.50
> *Margin Requirement:* $3,407.50
> *SMA Debit or Margin Call:* $3,407.50 - $837.50 = $2,570.00
> *Explanation:* Because the option is ITM, the margin requirement is 100% of the option proceeds plus 20% of the underlying security value. The sale proceeds may be applied to the initial margin requirement.

> **OTM short put position**
> Short 1 Sep 80 put at 2
> Underlying security at 95
>
> *Margin Calculation:* 100 x 2 = $ 200.00 *(A=100% option proceeds)*
> 20% x 100 x 95 = $ 1,900.00   *(B=20% of the underlying security value)*
> (95 - 80) x 100 = $(1,500.00)   *(C=OTM amount)*
> *(D=A+B-C=)* $ 600.00
> Therefore, minimum applies: 100 x 2 = $ 200.00   *(A)*
> 10% x 80 x 100 = 800.00   *(E=10% of strike price)*
> *(F=A+E=)* $1,000.00
> *Margin Requirement*: $1,000.00
> *SMA Debit or Margin Call*: $1,000.00 - $200.00 = $800.00
> *Explanation:* The margin requirement is 100% of the option proceeds plus 20% of the underlying security value less out-of-the-money amount, if any, to a minimum for puts of option proceeds plus 10% of the put's exercise price. The minimum applies in this example because the resulting margin requirement is greater than that of the basic formula. The sale proceeds may be applied to the initial margin requirement.

Instead of doing the calculation yourself, you can use the margin calculator on CBOE's website, which may be a good approximate of the actual margin requirements of your broker, if the broker adopts CBOE's formulae.

You can see from the margin formulae and the examples that, for selling call options, the margin is positively related to the price of the option and the price of the underlying stock, and negatively related to the amount that the option is out of money. The more the option is out of money, the less is the margin required for a short call option position, but the minimum amount is never less than 10% of the current value of the **underlying stock**. The higher is the current value of the underlying stock, the bigger the loss would be to the option writer.

For put option writing, the minimum margin amount is at least 10% of the **strike price**. The higher is the strike price, the more likely would the option writing make a loss.

Margin requirement is calculated on a daily basis, using the closing price of the underlying stock at the end of the trading day. If the previously calculated margin is less than the current margin calculated with the new stock closing price, then additional margin has to be posted. If there is inadequate margin in your brokerage account, your broker can liquidate your assets, such as stocks or bonds in order to bring the margin back to the required level.

If you trade complex option strategies, you will be trading multiple options at the same time. As if the calculation is not complex enough, margin requirements could be different from the sum of the margin requirements of individual options. The simple rule is that, for the same underlying stock, if you trade options that represent opposite views on the direction of the stock price (yes it is possible and can be profitable to do so) and they have the same expiration date, then the total margin requirement could be less than the sum of the margin requirements of individual options. Check with your broker to confirm, though.

For those who trade naked short options, managing margin position is an integral part of the trading process. You will have to think ahead to prevent a forced cancellation of positions, which could be ugly. Your broker could close positions according to their criteria even though you would have preferred something else. It would be better that you set a threshold level of your balance available for margin requirements, so that when that level is breached, you would take actions to bring it back to a comfortable level to meet adverse events.

4 IMPORTANT FACTORS THAT AFFECT OPTION VALUE

Current price of underlying stock and Delta

Unsurprisingly, option value is substantially affected by the current price of the underlying stock. More precisely, the impact of the current stock price on option value is derived from the distance of the current stock price from the strike price. The effect of the change in option value as a result of a change in the underlying stock price is captured by a ratio called Delta.

When the price of the underlying stock is moving slowly, delta can be used to estimate the option price based on the movement of the stock price. This is the main use of delta as far as individual/retail investors are concerned.

Delta is defined as the change in option value as a result of a one dollar (or unit) change (NOT percentage change) in the price of the underlying stock, when other factors (mainly volatility, risk free interest rate, time to expiration) remain almost the same, or change only a little. It is given a value that lies between 1 and -1. (An alternative convention multiplies that value by 100, changing the range from 100 to -100.) Call options have positive delta, and put options have negative delta. For a 0.15-delta option, if the underlying stock moves by $1, the option's per share value is expected to change by 15 cents. The short positions of these options have the opposite values, that is, the seller of a 0.15-delta call option is said to have -0.15 delta. In short, options with high delta value in absolute terms are more sensitive to stock price movements than low delta options.

For a small stock price movement, provided the other factors do not change much, delta can be used to give a good estimate of where option value price will be in the very near future. You can calculate historical delta value using the previous change in stock price and the actual change in option value, but expected delta value, which is what investors want to know to help them figure out where option price will be, can be calculated by using a mathematical model that takes into account some of the factors that affect an option's value (See box).

Delta is also viewed by some people as the probability of an option finishing in the money on expiration. A 30-delta option is said to have a 30% chance of finishing in the money. Others disagree, saying that this is mathematically incorrect. I do not have the mathematical training to take either side, but I can understand the appeal of thinking about delta in this way. Let us consider the question: if the current stock price is $100, what is the chance that it will go above $100 tomorrow? If stock price movement is random, then it would seem reasonable to say that it will have 50% chance of going up, and 50% chance of going down. If the current stock price is $110, then, assuming that stock price changes are normally distributed, we would agree that the chance of the stock price getting above $100 tomorrow is higher than 50% (the chance of the stock price getting above $110 tomorrow is already 50%). Delta of a call option is also higher when the stock price is higher than the strike price. When the stock price is below the strike price, then the chance that it will be above the strike price tomorrow would be less than 50%. Delta is also lower when the stock price is less than the strike price.

Does delta go up the same amount when the stock price goes from $100 to $110, as when the stock price goes from $110 to $120 for the same option? The answer is no. The value of delta is dependent on how far the current stock price is relative to the strike price, and how much time is left. Delta is 1 when the current stock price is so far above the strike price that it is nearly certain that, by the time the option expires, the call option would be in the money. When that point is reached, delta does not go up any more, no matter how much higher the stock price goes. Similarly, if the stock price goes far below the strike price of a call option, it would be safe to say that it is nearly impossible that, if the normal range of movement of stock price continues, the stock price at expiration would move up high enough to reach the strike price. At such point, delta would be zero. Even lower stock prices would not change delta any more since it is not possible for delta to go below zero. In theory, a gain in the price of underlying stock cannot lead to a fall in call option price if the other parameters do not change much. Negative delta is reserved for put options, where higher stock prices will lead to lower option value, and short call position, where any gain in the value of a long call position would be a corresponding loss in the short call position.

To give an idea of the typical values of delta, we present a table below which used the Black-Scholes model to generate theoretical delta value of a call option for a stock that is currently trading at $100 for various strike prices with different expiration dates, while volatility for the underlying stock is assumed to be the same at 25%.

Table: Theoretical call option delta values for a stock that is currently trading at $100 with volatility of 25% and riskless interest rate of 2%

	Strike at $80	Strike at $100	Strike at $120
60 days to expire	0.9895	0.533	0.0419
186 days to expire	0.9199	0.558	0.1884
305 days to expire	0.8789	0.5741	0.2703
550 days to expire	0.8372	0.5991	0.3658

The take-away:

1. Delta changes most rapidly when the current stock price is around the strike price of an option. At that price region, a small change in stock price can lead to a larger change in option value than that associated with the same amount of stock price movement when the stock price was far away from the strike price.

2. Most of the time during the life of an option, delta is around 0.5 when the current stock price is close to the strike price of an option. It only reaches 1 when the option is within days of expiring. Hence, an investor should not expect the value of an ATM option to move on a 1 to 1 scale except when the option is near expiration, contrary to what seems to be suggested by the options payoff equation.

Do these points hold for the delta values shown in the graph below?

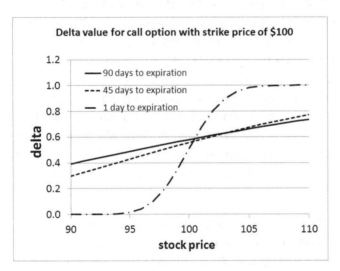

The graph shows the value of delta of a call option with strike price of $100. The risk free interest rate used in the equation is 8%, volatility is 45%, and no stock dividend (the importance of these parameters will be explained in later sections). For a call option with only one day to expire, delta is seen increasing rapidly as the call option moves from ATM to ITM, i.e. in this case when the stock price exceeds $100, the strike price. Option price becomes much more sensitive to stock price movements.

When the option has more time to go, say 45 days or 90 days, delta of an ATM call option does not change as fast as that of options with a shorter time to expiration. On the other hand, the actual delta value of an ATM call option that has more time to go can be higher when the stock price is below the strike price. See the delta value of the three options when stock price is, say, at $95. The opposite is true when the stock price is above the strike price. What the graphs are saying is this: as a call option approaches expiration, if the stock price is below the strike price, the option value will become less sensitive to changes in stock price; if the stock price is above the strike price, the option value will become more sensitive to changes in stock price.

Delta is particularly important for people who constantly have to neutralize the risk brought about by having open options positions. These are most likely people working in financial institutions which make money mainly from selling products to their clients, i.e. earning service fees, rather than from making directional bets on stock or options movements.

For these professionals, it is convenient to use delta as a unit for measuring the impact of a stock price change on the overall trade position. Each share of stock owned can be said to have a delta value of 1, because it is by definition the change in the value of a trade position that a one dollar movement of stock price brings. If someone has bought 5 put options, each with delta of -0.25, then that person is said to have delta position value of 5 times 100 times -0.25, which is -125. For every one dollar the stock price goes up, the value of the put options will drop by 125 dollars. Hence, to avoid losing money on the position, the seller would have to find ways to obtain +125 delta. He/she can do this by buying 125 shares of the underlying stock, or buying equivalent futures position on the stock. When the delta value of the overall position is zero, this condition is called delta neutral (See Box 4). He can even create the long delta positions synthetically, by combining options with short stock or futures positions.

Box 3   Delta is a ratio of changes in percentage, not ratio of percentage changes

Delta is the estimated change in the value of an option in response to a change of one unit in the value of the underlying stock. You can say that Delta is the change in option value as a percentage of one unit change in stock price. It does not measure the percentage change in value of the option price against the percentage change of the underlying stock price.

For example, if the price of a stock was $3 and one of its call options traded at $0.9 at that time, and if the option had delta of 0.45, then, if the stock price goes up by $1, the call option's per share value is estimated to go up by $0.45, to

---

$1.35. We can say that the change in option value is 45 percent of the change in stock price. In terms of percentage change against their original values, the stock price's increase was 33% while the option value is estimated to increase by 50%, which is 1.51 times the change of the stock price.

Delta value of put option is the complement value of a corresponding call option, with a negative sign. The absolute delta value of a put option with the same strike price and expiration of a call option has the value that, if added to the delta value of the call option, will come to 1.

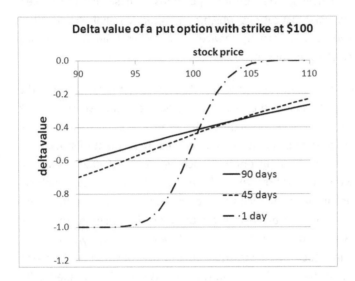

From the graph above, you can see that, when stock price is slightly above the strike of $100, the 45 day to expire put option has delta of -0.4. A call option with the same expiration and strike price for the same underlying stock will have a delta value of 0.6.

While a long put option position has negative delta, a short put option position has positive delta. Similarly, a long call option has positive delta, while a short call option position has negative delta. This means we can use either a long put or a short call option to obtain negative delta. If we want to profit from falling stock price, we can make use of a negative delta position, so that when the stock price goes down, the option value will go up.

However, the delta of the two types of options changes differently when stock price continues to go down. For a long put option position, the lower the stock price goes, the higher is the absolute value of the negative delta, i.e. the option price will go up more for the same dollar decline in stock price as the stock price continues to go lower. This is referred to as positive gamma. Gamma measures the change in the absolute value of delta in response to one unit change in stock price. A short call position, on the other hand, has negative gamma. As the stock price goes lower, the price of the call option also goes lower due to negative delta, increasing the gain to the option writer. However, the magnitude of the decrease in option value is less than before when the stock price continues to drop. After option value drops to zero, further decline in stock price will have no effect on the call option's price and delta has reached its minimum value of zero.

Box 4   Delta neutral

Delta neutral is a term that refers to the condition when the total delta position of a trade, which may comprise of just options or options and stocks, is zero. Under this condition, a small change in the price of the underlying asset will not have any effect on the total value of the trade position. For example, if a trade position is comprised of a long stock position of 100 shares (total delta equals +100) and options with total delta value of -100, then the total delta value of the position is zero. A 1 dollar gain in stock price will be offset by a decline in the value of the options positions by 1 dollar.

Why do some traders set up positions that have a combined delta value of zero? One reason is that those are traders, such as market makers, that do not want to take any risk, but only want income from trade commissions.

Others may want to profit from the impact of other factors on options value, such as changes in vega or interest rate, and do not want such gains to be adversely affected by movement in stock price.

Volatility and Vega

Volatility is very important for options trading. In fact, the profit opportunities offered by volatility movement is the main attraction of option trading. It is therefore worthwhile for us to spend a little more time on the subject.

Volatility in the context of options refers to the movement of the stock price's return from one day to the next, which is then annualized and presented in percentage term. The stock price's return is the percentage change in the closing price of the stock as compared to that on the previous trading day. The actual formula for calculating the statistical volatility of a stock price is a little bit more complicated than can be described in one sentence, but suffice to say that it is solely based on the magnitude of the historical changes in stock price.

The normal, quiet day, volatility of a mid cap stock is about 25% (i.e. the annualized return was between +25% and -25% from the mean return about 68% of the time, since volatility is one standard deviation). When the market is in a frenzy or panic, volatility can go up to 45% or even higher. For small cap stocks and growth stocks, the range of volatility can be greater still.

Below is a diagram showing the theoretical value of a call option that has a strike price of $100 and 45 days to expiration (risk free interest rate of 8%). The two lines on the diagram plot stock price against option value at different volatilities, the higher one has a volatility of 90%, and the lower one 45%. It can be seen that the option value can change quite dramatically if volatility suddenly goes up or down substantially. In this example, the theoretical option value more than doubles when volatility doubles and when stock price is far below the strike price of $100 (because of smaller original value).

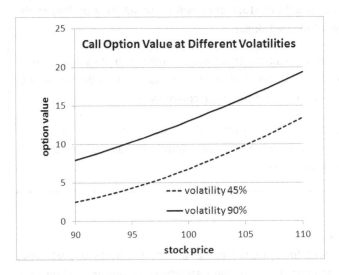

To show you the impact of different volatilities on option value as stock price changes, we show you the percentage change in option value in the table below:

stock price (strike is $100)	90	95	100	105	110
Option value at volatility	2.49	4.31	6.77	9.85	13.47

45%					
Option value at volatility 90%	7.89	10.27	12.99	16.02	19.32
% increase	216.34%	138.50%	91.90%	62.59%	43.43%

Below is a graph of GOOG's stock price volatility from April to November 2011 obtained from a free volatility calculator downloaded from www.softpedia.com. Notice how volatility can drop rapidly when the stock price trades in a small range, as in the periods marked by the circles in the graph.

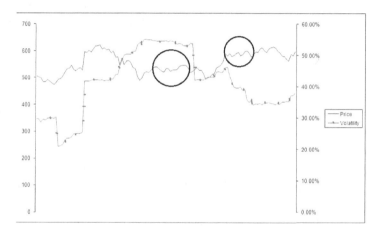

Options traders prefer to look at implied volatility, which is the level of volatility as calculated from option pricing formulae. These formulae usually use volatility as one of the inputs. Instead of using a historical volatility and other inputs to obtain a theoretical option value, investors can reverse a formula, use option price as an input, and obtain an implied volatility, which shows the level of volatility that is already priced into the option price. In other words, implied volatility shows what the market expects volatility to be in future. If the investor thinks that actual volatility would be higher than the volatility implied in the option price, then he/she can buy an option now, and profit from a higher option value later. If he/she thinks that the actual volatility would be lower, then he/she can sell an option now, and profit from a lower option value later.

Take home:

When volatility rises, option price goes up. When volatility goes down, option price goes down. This happens because traders believe that higher volatility will increase the chance of the stock price reaching a higher or lower value than it was yesterday. Hence, the value of both call and put options goes up when volatility goes up.

Volatility smile/skew

In theory (e.g. Black-Scholes model), the relationship between implied volatility and strike price is assumed to be constant. In practice, it has been observed, especially after 1987, during a period of high volatility, implied volatility changes with strike price. Sometimes, a graph showing the relationship between implied volatility and strike price is curve that looks like a smile, with implied volatility at the lowest when the strike price equals the current price of the underlying stock, and higher for strike prices that are further away from the current stock price. A volatility/strike price graph of such shape is called a volatility smile. More common for stock options that are close to expiration, however, are graphs of a shape that is called a skew. For call options, the graph will most likely be a downward slope from left to right, that is, implied volatility becomes lower the higher are the strike price. In turn, this means that as an option becomes OTM, implied volatility goes down.

Some option traders interpret a skewed, instead of flat, volatility /strike price graph as representing the demand for options for particular strike prices. Higher implied volatility for call options with lower strike is said to mean higher demand for ITM options. This is regarded as a sign that investors hold bullish view about the long term future of the underlying stock.

For put options, the skew, which is a upward slope from the left to the right of the graph, shows higher implied volatility for OTM options. This is interpreted to mean higher demand for OTM options, and this is further interpreted to mean that investors are worried about the possibility of a market crash in the near future.

How accurate are these interpretations is unknown. There may be more factors at play than meets the eye, such as technically driven market demand (e.g. demand from index funds when they need to gain exposure but would like to limit capital outlay). For retail investors, we should look for trading opportunities with wide 'moat' as they say, which means high expected profit, so that we do not need to worry about errors in such interpretations. Put simply, I would not advise retail options investors to pay too much attention to volatility smile/skew.

Vega

The same change in volatility does not have the same impact on options of different strike prices. For traders who need to distinguish small differences in the impact of volatility, vega is the number that they will monitor.

Vega (by the way is a Latin not a Greek word) measures the dollar change in the price of an option for a one percent movement in implied volatility. Vega is presented as the dollar amount in cents. A 5 vega option has a 5-cent vega. If an option that has a price of $5 at an implied volatility of 40% and a vega of 8, then when the implied volatility increases to 41%, theoretically the option value will increase by (41-40) times 8 cents. That means, theoretically, the option value is expected to increase to $5.08.

Vega is highest at the money and decreases as the stock price moves away from the strike price in either direction.

Vega is higher for options of the same strike price that have a further expiration date than ones that are closer to expiration. In other words, vega decreases with the passage of time.

When is vega useful? When you want to choose between two similar options, and volatility is expected to change significantly before you would close the position. The option with a higher vega will have a larger change in option value than one with a lower vega for the same change in volatility. If you want to get a large impact from volatility, you would choose the option whose strike price is closer to the current stock price, or has more time to expiration. If your strategy depends on a reduction of impact from volatility, you would choose an option that is not too close to expiration, so as to benefit from the drop in vega over time.

From the graph below, which uses vega value obtained from the Black-Scholes model for a call option, it can be seen that, options with longer time to expire are more sensitive to changes in volatility than options that are about to expire.

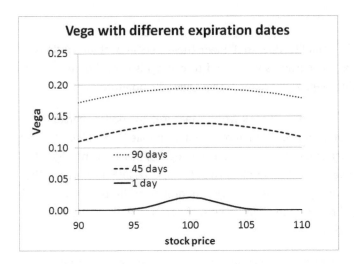

The next graph shows vega value for different strike prices, for call options with one day to expiration.

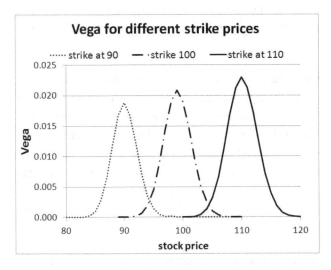

Put options will have similar graphs. Vega is highest when the option is ATM.

Time decay and theta

We covered the term 'time value' of an option earlier. To recap, it is the difference between the price of an option and its intrinsic value. The intrinsic value, in turn, is the value of an option as defined by its payoff equation: for a call option, it equals to the stock price minus the strike price if the stock price is higher than the strike price; for a put option, it equals to the strike price minus the stock price if the strike price is higher than the stock price. The time value is large when there is a lot of time left until the option expires, and it becomes smaller as expiration approaches. This decrease in the time value as a result of the passing of time is called time decay.

Time decay occurs because the probability of an out-of-money option becoming in the money decreases as an option gets closer to expiration.

Time decay is most rapid in the last 30 days of an option's life. This means that, theta, which represents the rate of time decay, is higher in the last 30 days than when, say, there were 45 days left. Theta will continue to move higher as expiration approaches. Since theta represents a fall in option value, it has a negative sign. A theta of -0.05 means that an option would likely decline by $0.05 the next day.

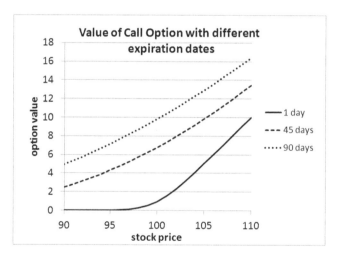

The graph above shows the theoretical value of a call option with strike price at $100 (with risk free rate of 8%, volatility of 45% and no dividend) with different time to expiration. Since time value is the difference between option value and intrinsic value, we can subtract intrinsic value from the option value to get the time value. When the stock price is below $100, say at $90, all the option value is time value. Intrinsic value can be read from an option's payoff graph, and the value of a call option with only one day to expire is very similar to the shape of the payoff graph. Using this information, we can see that when the option has 90 days to expiration and the stock price is below $100, its time value is highest among the three options. Time value is reduced to almost zero when the option has only one day left.

When an option is very deep in the money (eg. When stock price is 50% above strike price of a call option), on the other hand, it has little or no time value, so time decay is not much of a problem.

Intuitively, this makes sense, since the option is so deep in the money that there is only a small chance that it will become out of the money. In such cases, only the intrinsic value should matter.

When an option has only one day to expire, its theoretical value at various stock prices is similar to the payoff graph of the option, i.e. if the stock price is $105, then the option value of a call option would be about $5, since the strike price ($100) is below the stock price by about that amount.

The last two paragraphs tell you that, if we extend the stock price shown in the above diagram to beyond $110, the three graphs representing different time to expiration will converge when stock price is very high.

If your strategy is to gain from appreciation in option value, as in the holding of a long option position, then theta is your enemy, especially in the last 30 days of the option's life, because time will always pass. Conversely, if you have written an option, as such your strategy depends on a drop in option value, then theta is a friend. These will become very clear in the next chapter when individual strategies are explained.

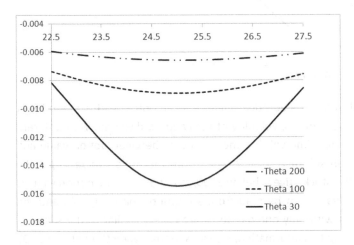

The above graph shows the value of Theta (vertical axis) for call options with different strike prices and different number of days (30 days, 100 days and 200 days) to expire. The current stock price is $25.

Apart from the Greeks, there are two more major factors that influence option value.

Dividends

Some stocks pay cash dividend to their shareholders. Whoever is the stock owner on record before the ex-dividend date will receive the dividend a few days after that date. Stock price of such stocks usually drops by the amount of the dividend immediately after the ex-dividend date. Call option holders of such stocks, however, will not receive dividends. Call option prices are therefore expected to fall immediately after the ex-dividend date, while put option prices are expected to go up.

Similarly, since option pricing models usually assume that options are exercised only upon expiry and that if dividend paid any time before that would be received by the call option writer rather than the call option holder, call option premium is lower than if the underlying stock does not pay cash dividend.

Interest rate

It is commonly believed that, if interest rate is high, call option premiums will be higher than if interest rate is low, but put option premiums will be lower. When interest rate is high, investors will be happy to buy call options instead of stocks and make the same gain when stock prices go up, because they can deposit the cash saved in an interest earning account. Most options valuation models also assume a direct relationship between call option price and interest rate.

Compared with shorting stocks, buying put options would be less attractive when interest rate is high, since the proceeds from shorting stocks could be used to earn interest.

In sum, these factors and their derivative "Greeks" like delta, vega and theta are useful as a guide to help us determine the likely movement in option prices. However, actual option price movements are less predictable than we would like. Market imperfections such as low trading volume, gaps in strike prices available, information asymmetry, and in fact just simple behavioral dynamics of different groups of investors can contribute to erratic option price movements. Therefore, even after using the Greeks as guides, we should also give a wide margin of safety in trading options to increase our odds of success.

Since there is more than one factor at work at any one time during the life of an option, we are often required to decide which factor should we focus our attention on, in order to choose the optimal strategy. The answer could be different for different circumstances. In general, the impact of volatility and price of the underlying stock, followed by time decay, would be larger than factors such as interest rate and dividend.

Greek values

If we focus our efforts on a number of familiar stocks to trade options, we can get a general idea of the Greek values from free options calculators, and usually that is sufficient for retail investors like us. However, if we want to have tools to help us find options that meet certain criteria, there are sites that provide live data on Greek values for a fee:

http://www.ivolatility.com
http://www.optionistics.com
http://www.optionetics.com

---

5   BASIC OPTION STRATEGIES

Planning ahead

Before we dive into specific option strategies, I would like new option investors to think about a couple of matters first. One is the need for a plan, and two is our trading psychology.

When we see a trading opportunity or a need to trade for protection or other purposes, we will experience an urge to immediately enter into a position. For example, when the market has been moving down very fast recently, we would feel that we need to do something to protect our existing position (fear), or to position ourselves to gain from that trend (greed).

At the same time that we decide on trading an option, we should have a plan that details what to do in different situations before and on option expiration. We need to decide before hand what to do if the market goes our way, when it goes against us, and when it is unpredictable, since option value can change very fast. If you do not have a plan, you are unlikely to make the best response when the time comes. To help us execute our exit strategies, we could use stop or stop limit orders. Some options platform can offer more sophisticated exit or position adjustment strategies, and you can get more information from your broker.

Even more than stock trading, successful options trading require us to give a margin of safety when we plan our trade. This means that, before entering a trade, the estimated potential profit must be higher than what you are willing to take for the level of risk associated with that trade. When the trade is going your way, do not try to wait for the maximum profit to occur, but exit when you have captured, say, 80% of that. When the trade is going against you, estimate the chances of your position getting back to the black, discount that value by 30%, and see if you would still want to keep the position open. Unexpected adverse events occur more often than we would like, and for retail investors, due to our limited access to information as compared to institutional investors, the unexpected events occur even more frequent.

For some option types, like buying call options, the options pricing has a built-in margin of safety, which is that when the stock price goes up, the at the money call option will become in the money and the out of money call option will become closer to be in the money, and delta will theoretically go up, so that even if the stock price goes up less than we expected, option value can increase far enough for us to make a profit. Even so, for options with low trading volume and open positions, we should increase the margin of safety, so as to absorb some costs due to market 'imperfection'.

A list of essential decisions to make before entering a trade should contain at least the following:

- How much is the potential profit and how likely we can get it
- How long are we prepared to stay in the trade
- How much should we allocate to the trade
- How much loss we are willing to bear

Between potential profit and probability of realizing that profit, I believe more weight should be given to the probability factor, and no trade should be initiated with a probability of success of less than 60%, since that number is often nothing more than our best guesstimate.

Whether trading stocks or options, we are essentially trying to make money from taking a view on the future of a financial product. That view may come true only at a particular time in future, but we often do not know exactly when. Before that happens, the value of our trade could move in the wrong direction. If we review the situation and still believe that the view that we had is still valid, do we have enough time and resources to withstand the adversity before we are proven correct? Even if we do, would that be wise? Because option value can change very fast, we need to be prepared for a worst case scenario before entering the trade.

How much should we allocate to a trade depends on the purpose of a trade as well as our overall equity portfolio management objectives. If we use long option positions to protect existing stock position, for example, do we want to hedge the whole position, knowing that the cost would be very high, or partially to the extent of our risk tolerance? Even though we may not always have the exact answer, we need to bear these issues in mind. One of the important rules is that the amount allocated to options could be higher if the downside risk is lower, and vice versa. Long option positions could be allocated more capital than short option positions, since the maximum loss is limited and predetermined for long positions but not short positions.

Finally, we should not underestimate the effect of emotions on our trading decisions. Do we tend to sell quickly on the first sight of loss, or hang on to a position all the way to the end in the hope of a recovery? Make an effort to review the trading records and try to figure out what we could have done better, knowing what we knew at that time. It is hard to go against our built-in emotions, but we can find ways to compensate, or even use them, if we take time to know our own trading psychology.

Now we are ready to look at option trading strategies. I have included below the most often seen option strategies. I will go into more detail on the first five strategies because once you understand these strategies, you can superimpose their analysis on more complicated strategies that are built from these most basic ones. In fact, I think using simple strategies (i.e. those employing no more than two types of options) well can capture most of the benefits that are available from option trading already. Just because a strategy requires very complicated set up does not mean that the benefit is proportionally bigger. There are trade-offs for using complicated options strategies.

i.   Simple Long Call

A long call refers to a strategy in which the investor intends to make profit by buying a call option, the payoff of which is directly related to the movement of the price of the underlying stock, as long as the stock price is above the exercise price. As can be seen from the payoff equation of a long call, the maximum that one can lose is the option premium. The maximum amount that you could gain is theoretically unlimited as there is no law that caps how high a stock price can go.

When stock price looks set to rise, investors would be tempted to buy call options to profit from the stock movement. Imagine the high profit we can make, by just using a fraction of the cash required for share purchase! This is in fact the time when we are most vulnerable, as we could be tempted to buy a call option without proper planning. Paying too much for an option could mean that even when we correctly predicted the direction of the stock price, our option trade ends up making significant losses.

In order to make profit on a long call position, our focus should be on the potential increase in option value, and not just on the potential gain in underlying stock price as implied in the payoff equation, as stock price is only one of the many factors that affect option value. We can get a decent increase in option value only when (i) we can buy the option at a low premium; and (ii) the option value is expected to go much higher after we bought it. A common mistake is for an investor to focus too much on (ii), and ignore (i).

When will the option premium of a call option be low? When volatility is low, and the market expects the stock price to go down or stay flat at best.

Another reference point to check whether an option price is low or not, is to compare its time value to the potential gain in option value. If you recall, time value is the difference between an option's current price and its intrinsic value. Intrinsic value for a call option, in turn, is current stock price minus strike price. For an out-of-money (OTM) option, all the value of an option is time value.

For example, for a call option with a strike price of $20 and the underlying stock at $28, it has an intrinsic value of $8. If the option price is over $8, then this excess value is the time value. If the strike price for the option is $30, then it has no intrinsic value, and all of the option value is time value, since the current stock price is below the strike price. Time value will decrease in value as expiration approaches, and falls to zero when expiration is very near. If we buy options with a time value and are prepared to hold it to expiration, then the stock price will have to rise more than the time value to make any profit. If the option with strike at $20 and underlying stock price at $28 is selling for $11, then the time value is $3. If the option is to be profitable, assuming the option is sufficiently deep ITM and near enough to expiration for delta to be around 1, then stock price has to rise above $31.

If we buy OTM call options, the stock price will have to rise even more for the option to be profitable before expiration, since delta of OTM call options is lower than one, and $1 increase in stock price will only lead to a less than $1 increase in option value. If an option with strike of $45 is selling at $5 and has a delta of 0.3 when the stock price is at $40, it has a time value of $5 (since option is OTM). A $1 rise in stock price will lead to only $0.3 increase in option value. Even though delta will increase as the stock price increases and the option becomes closer to be in-the-money, the stock price will have to rise a lot more than the time value for the option value to increase sufficiently to make a profit. Hence, high time value relative to the potential gain in stock price is a sign that the option price could be too high.

Low option price on its own is not sufficient to make option trading successful. Buying an option is to enter a race against time. As time passes, the option loses value. Thus, we need to identify with sufficient confidence a situation whereby the option price will rise in a meaningful way within the life span of an option before buying that option.

Option price can make large jumps (a) when delta is high and stock price moves up; and (b) when stock price increases in volatility, e.g. a 10% move within a day.

Option delta is high (say, above 0.7) when an option is deep in the money (ITM), and close to expiration. When an option has more time to expiration, the option has to be deeper in the money for delta to be near 1. For example, an option with three months to expire could have a delta at 0.9 when its underlying stock price is 200% above the strike price. When it has only ten days to expire, the stock price needs to be only 10% above the strike price for delta to be the same.

This and time decay are the reasons why we should normally buy call options with shorter expiration than ones with longer time to expire, as long as the expiration is not too short as to be less than 30 days when time decay is fastest. For example, if you expect the price of a stock to go up significantly in the next 30 days, then you should buy call options that have no more than 60 days to expire. You can then exit the position when the option still has at least 30 days to expire.

We will show an example of how to profit from deep ITM call option, where delta is high. When delta is low, it is also possible to make profit, but we have to be more nimble and careful. We will illustrate this in another example.

As regards the effect of volatility, here is an example. Google's stock price dropped about 20% in from April to June 2011, due to obscure reasons such as the new CEO did not spend much time explaining the company's direction, and concerns about its new initiatives. It then bounced back from 475 to 620 in July 2011 due to better than expected results.

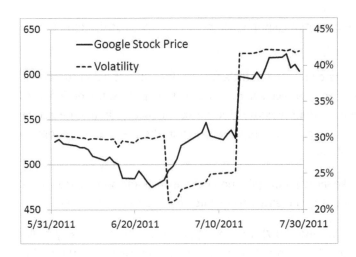

The above diagram shows the stock price and volatility of Google in the months of June and July 2011. The price of a Google call option that expires on 21 January 2012 at a strike of $750 is plotted in the diagram below for the same period. When the stock price moved from $528 to $597 (+12%) on 15 July 2011, the option price shot up from $1.994 to reach $6.017 (+201%). Part of that leap in option price could be attributed to delta, which would be around 0.03 and probably was responsible for (0.03 x $69) $2 of the increase in option price, but the rest of the impact came from the increase in volatility, which changed from 25% to 40% overnight, and significantly increased the chances of the option to be in the money before expiration.

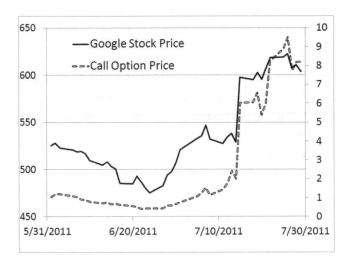

LEAPS

Since option value diminishes with time, we should buy options with expiration just long enough for our strategy to work out. This is particularly true when we are considering options with expiration of below one year: buying long option positions with a further out expiration date is usually more expensive than buying those with nearer expiration date. However, for very long dated options, such as those called LEAPS, Long Term Anticipation Securities, which can expire beyond one year, once in a while, you can pick up relatively cheap options.

Below is a table listing Microsoft Corporation (MSFT) options on 14 July 2011. Its share price was at $26.63.

Options   Get Option

View By Expiration: Jul 11 | Aug 11 | Sep 11 | Oct 11 | **Jan 12** | Apr 12 | Jan 13

Call Options   Expire at close Friday, January 20, 2012

Strike	Symbol	Last	Chg	Bid	Ask	Vol	Open Int
12.50	MSFT120121C00012500	13.14	0.00	N/A	N/A	2	562
15.00	MSFT120121C00015000	11.87	0.00	N/A	N/A	4	4,598
17.50	MSFT120121C00017500	9.22	0.00	N/A	N/A	2	6,430
20.00	MSFT120121C00020000	6.75	0.00	N/A	N/A	90	24,073
21.00	MSFT120121C00021000	5.90	0.00	N/A	N/A	13	3,366
22.50	MSFT120121C00022500	4.65	0.00	N/A	N/A	74	62,925
24.00	MSFT120121C00024000	3.32	0.00	N/A	N/A	50	52,777
25.00	MSFT120121C00025000	2.63	0.00	N/A	N/A	559	129,997
26.00	MSFT120121C00026000	2.02	0.00	N/A	N/A	346	32,291
27.50	MSFT120121C00027500	1.28	0.00	N/A	N/A	16,792	145,986
29.00	MSFT120121C00029000	0.74	0.00	N/A	N/A	2,210	25,571

Source: Yahoo! Finance

The above table shows prices of MSFT call options that would expire in January 2012. The tables below shows call options that would expire one year later. Both sets of options are LEAPS, and so are the options that would expire in April 2012. When they were created, they had at least one year to expire.

View By Expiration: Jul 11 | Aug 11 | Sep 11 | Oct 11 | Jan 12 | Apr 12 | **Jan 13**

Call Options						Expire at close Friday, January 18, 2013	
Strike	Symbol	Last	Chg	Bid	Ask	Vol	Open Int
12.50	MSFT130119C00012500	14.25	0.00	N/A	N/A	20	2,476
15.00	MSFT130119C00015000	11.56	0.00	N/A	N/A	8	2,639
17.50	MSFT130119C00017500	9.26	0.00	N/A	N/A	67	6,496
20.00	MSFT130119C00020000	7.25	0.00	N/A	N/A	53	26,282
22.50	MSFT130119C00022500	5.27	0.00	N/A	N/A	78	35,309
25.00	MSFT130119C00025000	3.60	0.00	N/A	N/A	11,416	138,297
27.00	MSFT130119C00027000	2.60	0.00	N/A	N/A	42	8,138
28.00	MSFT130119C00028000	2.38	0.00	N/A	N/A	7,505	1,528
30.00	MSFT130119C00030000	1.50	0.00	N/A	N/A	1,666	190,571
32.50	MSFT130119C00032500	0.96	0.00	N/A	N/A	6	65,464
35.00	MSFT130119C00035000	0.58	0.00	N/A	N/A	106	92,291

Source: Yahoo! Finance

On 14 July 2011, Microsoft (MSFT) was trading at $26.63. Notice how small the differences are for options with strike price at $17.50 and below. For example, for a deep in the money strike of $15, the option expiring in January 2012 costs $11.87, while the one expiring in January 2013 costs $11.56 (even lower!).

If we buy the January 2013 call option with strike of $15 when the stock price is at $26.63, the intrinsic value is $11.63. If we could buy it at the last traded option price of $11.56, then we would actually be PAID $0.08 to own the Microsoft shares. Of course, it is also possible that the last traded price was out dated, and the current price could be higher. Also, the low LEAPS price could be contributed by the fact that MSFT is a dividend paying stock, and options holders do not receive the dividends. But MSFT's dividend yield at that point was only 2.4%, so the low option price was still very attractive.

If an investor had bought the $15 strike call option at $11.50, while MSFT closed at $26.47 on that day, he/she would have obtained the benefit of owning MSFT using only 11.5/26.47 (43%) of the capital required to buy the shares outright. Since delta for the option would be near 1, if MSFT goes up by $1 to $27.47 (+4%), the option value should also go up by $1, to $12.50 (+8.7%), a leverage of 2.3 times (which can also be obtained from inversing 43%).

An important question to ask before trading: why was MSFT option so cheap? In the previous 12 months, the stock price of MSFT had been trading in a narrow range of between $23 and $27 most of the time, the proverbial cold stock. It seems that the market did not expect it to go very high, and this causes the option price to be low. If the market is correct, then we could lose money on the long call option position. With the leverage from the call option, however, we can get a not so cold return even if the stock moves only a little, and we have a lot of time to review our bet.

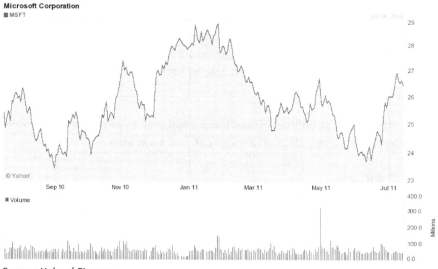

Source: Yahoo! Finance

Deep ITM call option

As can be seen in the above example, there are good reasons for buying deep in the money call options. In the event that the stock price goes up after buying the option, we do not have to watch delta, since delta has either reached its maximum value of one, or is moving towards one. We can now focus completely on stock price movement. If you have good reason to believe the stock price's ascend is coming to an end, or no good reason to believe that it will go up some more, you should not hesitate to sell your call option and lock in the profit. If you can sell it when volatility is high, then that would be a bonus for you, because the option price will be higher.

Taking profit is important in long option positions, first because of the large swing in option prices and second is time decay. Transaction cost should not be a consideration, unless you have an expensive broker. So do not feel bad after taking a 25% profit on a call option and then watch the option price going up another 25%. In the long run, you will see some call options that go higher after you sell, and some go lower also.

However, if you believe that the stock has long term prospect and will recover from any interim swings, buying a deep ITM call option allows you to purchase the shares at a low price. Say we bought the January 2012 MSFT call option with strike $15, and on expiration, the stock price were $14.50. The option will be exercised automatically, and we will pay $15 for the purchase of each share. The total cost of buying the share becomes $26.5 ($11.50 + $15). It may seem that we are paying higher than the market price for the shares, but for that price we had enjoyed the chance of obtaining leveraged profit for a period of time. Comparing buying the call option to buying the shares of MSFT in July 2011 at $26.47, the former is still a better choice.

Using a deep ITM call option is therefore a good way to obtain shares of solid companies that are going through a rough patch at a low price.

Far OTM options

Some people like to buy far out of money call options (i.e. options with strike price that are at least 20% above current stock price), because such options are cheaper. For example, on 29 September 2011, when Bank of America (BAC) closed at $6.35, its at-the-money $6 call option expiring in Dec 2011 cost $1.10, while the $7 out-of-money call option cost $0.59. The far out of money options at $9 cost only $0.13.

Options   Bank of America $6.35 on 29 Sep 2011   Get Options for:

View By Expiration: Sep 11 | Oct 11 | Nov 11 | **Dec 11** | Jan 12 | Feb 12 | May 12 | Dec 12 | Jan 13 | Dec 13

| Call Options | | | | | | | Expire at close Friday, December 16, 2011 |
Strike	Symbol	Last	Chg	Bid	Ask	Vol	Open Int
2.00	BAC111217C00002000	4.40	0.00	4.35	4.45	3	9
3.00	BAC111217C00003000	3.45	↓0.40	3.45	3.50	60	979
4.00	BAC111217C00004000	2.54	↓0.26	2.58	2.60	35	3,227
5.00	BAC111217C00005000	1.66	↑0.01	1.78	1.80	199	5,789
6.00	BAC111217C00006000	1.10	↑0.07	1.11	1.13	470	6,992
7.00	BAC111217C00007000	0.59	↑0.03	0.61	0.62	1,581	20,553
8.00	BAC111217C00008000	0.30	↑0.02	0.30	0.32	808	20,146
9.00	BAC111217C00009000	0.13	↓0.01	0.13	0.14	489	12,522
10.00	BAC111217C00010000	0.07	↑0.01	0.06	0.07	155	16,209
11.00	BAC111217C00011000	0.04	0.00	0.03	0.04	4	7,921
12.00	BAC111217C00012000	0.02	0.00	N/A	0.03	672	8,696

Source: Yahoo! Finance

While the delta for options with higher strike price is lower, because the initial value of the option is very small, the percentage gain if the stock price goes up by $1 is pretty impressive, as can be seen from the table below, if the theoretical delta value works out.

Table: Delta value based on 75 days to expiration, current stock price of $6.35, volatility of 45% and risk free rate of 2%

strike price	6.00	7.00	8.00	9.00
delta	0.655	0.500	0.156	0.056
current option value	1.100	0.590	0.300	0.130
new value if stock goes up $1	1.755	1.090	0.456	0.186
% change in option value	59.59%	84.75%	52.06%	43.22%

Note that if an option is out of money, unlike deep in the money options, delta is higher when the option has more time to expire. The corresponding deltas for the above options with 120 days to expire are: 0.646, 0.412, 0.229 and 0.116, for example. So if you are going to buy far OTM options in anticipation of an imminent stock price appreciation, then you should buy longer dated ones.
Thus, it would seem that buying far OTM options is a good idea. However, we need to remember that potential gain is not only dependent on the potential rise in option value, but also the probability of that rise. A far OTM option has a small chance of being in the money on expiration.

BAC stock price did spike up after September. It reached $7.35 on 28 October. If an investor bought a $9 strike call option in September and sold it at the end of October, the trade probably would have been profitable. But not if it were sold later. On 5 December 2011, BAC share price closed at $5.79. The value of the December 17 call options with strikes at $7 and above became no more than $0.02.

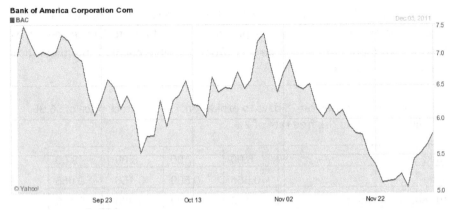

Bank of America Corporation Com
■ BAC

Dec 05, 2011

Sep 23   Oct 13   Nov 02   Nov 22

Source: Yahoo! Finance

Below is a table showing the price of BAC options on 5 December 2011. You will notice that for each strike price, there are two options. The date of expiration of each is different. Those expiring on 9 December(as can be read from the option symbol) would seem to be a new series introduced in November. Care should be taken in such cases so that we do not read the wrong price or trade the wrong options.

Call Options						Expire at close Thursday, December 8, 2011	
Strike	Symbol	Last	Chg	Bid	Ask	Vol	Open Int
1.00	BAC111217C00001000	4.30	0.00	4.75	4.80	206	206
2.00	BAC111217C00002000	3.85	↑0.55	3.75	3.80	31	6
3.00	BAC111217C00003000	2.75	↑0.05	2.76	2.80	124	1,731
4.00	BAC111209C00004000	1.80	↑0.10	1.76	1.80	206	386
4.00	BAC111217C00004000	1.77	↑0.09	1.79	1.81	702	7,990
5.00	BAC111209C00005000	0.78	↑0.10	0.79	0.81	3,956	6,261
5.00	BAC111217C00005000	0.83	↑0.10	0.83	0.84	12,428	50,632
6.00	BAC111209C00006000	0.09	0.00	0.08	0.09	22,750	20,773
6.00	BAC111217C00006000	0.16	0.00	0.16	0.17	32,945	230,063
7.00	BAC111209C00007000	0.01	0.00	N/A	0.01	190	1,608
7.00	BAC111217C00007000	0.02	↓0.01	0.02	0.03	11,347	262,767
8.00	BAC111217C00008000	0.01	0.00	N/A	0.01	1,385	88,827
9.00	BAC111217C00009000	0.01	0.00	N/A	0.01	21	69,062

Source: Yahoo! Finance

We should also note that, for out of money or even at the money call options, delta is expected to move lower faster than in the money call options as time goes by.

To make money buying far OTM options therefore means that you would have to monitor them closely and be prepared to close the positions long before expiration if they work out for you, but even more so when they do not.

On expiration

If you still own a call option on expiration, and it is in the money, then, unless your broker has special rules, your contract will be exercised automatically. You will be obliged to buy the stocks at the strike price. Your broker will deduct the money required from your account, and credit the stocks to your portfolio. Thus, you must make sure you have sufficient fund in your account on that day, else your broker will start charging you interest for the deficit.

To sum up, the best time to buy a call option is (i) when a company's stock price has been going nowhere, and you expect something good to happen to it in the not too distant future; and (2) when the company's stock price drops drastically due to some obscure bad news or temporary setback in your view.

Simple Long Call Risk and Reward Summary
Maximum profit: theoretically unlimited, as there is no limit to how high a stock's price can go. (It goes without saying that, for all option trades, net profit/loss has to take into account the cost of brokerage commission.) It occurs when the stock price is higher than the strike price plus costs.
Maximum loss: limited to option premium paid plus costs.
Waiting for option premium to drop before buying an option will greatly improve the chances of making a profit.

---

ii.   Simple Long Put

A simple long position in a put option is a bet on the increase in the value of an option whose payoff is negatively related to the price of a stock. Similar to a simple call option, a put option does not involve borrowed money, and the maximum amount that you could lose is the price of the option that you paid. The maximum amount that you could gain, on the other hand, is the strike price of the option, since payoff is only positive if the stock price is below the strike price, and the stock price cannot go below zero.

Same as with buying call options, we should aim to buy put options that could give us a big increase in option price with a reasonably good chance. A put option's price would be low when the stock price is moving higher steadily (i.e. volatility is low). If the time value is small, and you believe that stock price is going to go a lot lower, or go a little lower very fast, then you could buy a put option.

Delta of a long put, like long call, is higher when the put option is ITM than when it is OTM. As time passes, the delta of an ITM will go higher (approaches -1) , while that of an OTM will go lower (approaches 0). This means that, for a OTM long put option position, as time goes by, it will take greater stock price movement for option price to move higher.

Exercise

Since a put option buyer has the right to sell shares underlying the option at a pre-agreed price, when he/she chooses to exercise the option, he/she will have to deliver the shares while an amount equal to the number of shares time the strike price will be credited to his/her account. If the put option buyer does not own the shares underlying the option, then he/she may end up with a short position of the stock.

Example

Let us say you think stock ABC will drop in price significantly after earnings announcement because it had been overbought beforehand. It is currently trading at $40 per share, and you believe there is a good chance that it will go down to $30.

Let's say a put option with strike price of $40 is selling for $2 per share (all of it is time value). You would of course choose an option that will expire shortly after earnings announcement, since options usually cost more with longer expiration. If you buy options that have longer expiration than needed, it will cost more and as a result it will reduce your chances of making a profit.

For a put option that is at the money (ATM) with about 30 days to expire, delta is usually around -0.5, or slightly higher. However, that delta value is only valid for a small stock price change. As stock price falls, delta will increase (towards -1), which means that option value will rise faster. Once a put option is in the money, it will acquire intrinsic value. Let us assume that when stock price drops to $30, the option sells for $10.45, $10 of which is intrinsic. Your profit at this point is $8.45 ($10.45 - $2). To exit the position, you could simply set a sell limit order any time after you bought the put option. If your target profit level is $8.50, then your limit order sell price should be $10.50.

58

Alternatively, when the stock price drops to $30, since your put option would be in the money (ITM), you could exercise your option and sell the underlying stocks at $40. You will have $40 credited to your brokerage account, plus a short position of the stock if you did not own the shares before selling the shares. You can now buy back those stocks at the open market at $30. Your gain would be $10 per share from the trading of shares, minus $2 for the cost of the put option and commissions. Your profit would be $8 per share before commission. However, you will have to manually give instruction to exercise the option and buy the shares, unless your broker has very sophisticated options automation system.

From this example, you can see that the first way of trading i.e. selling the option, is more profitable than exercising the option. As long as there is time left, a long option position that is ITM will have some time value in addition to the intrinsic value.

The same alternative of exercising the option is available to call options.

To give another example, suppose at the end of July 2011, you think Google's share price would go down with the market in August. On 1 August, Google's share price closed at $606. A Google put option with strike at $480 that would expire on 21 January 2012 was selling for $9.13 (all time value). Since Google's share price had been volatile, you estimated that it could go down to $450 in the next six months if the market condition deteriorates. Assuming an average delta of -0.5, you projected that the option price could go up by ($150 x 0.5 =) $75, so you set the sell target at ($75 x 0.8 + $9.13=) $69.13, giving a safety margin of 20%. You also set a stop loss of 20%, so that the option would be sold if its value dropped by 20% or more from the purchase price.

Below are graphs showing the movement of stock price of Google and the put option in August 2011.

At first, your projection was correct. The stock price did go down. Your option had become profitable very fast.

Suppose on 25 August, you saw that Google's price started to go up. You changed your plan and decided to lock in the profit made so far, and sold your option at $31.8. Your profit is $31.8 - $9.13 = $22.67 per share. Below is a diagram showing the volatility and option price of Google for the same period. From the two diagrams, you can see how fast option price can fall once the stock price changes direction.

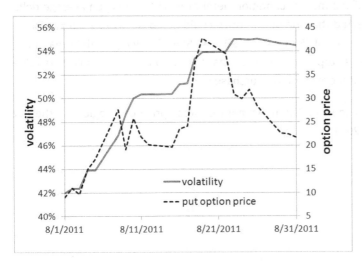

For those who have been reading this book carefully, I know you have a question: why the strike price? Indeed, it would have been more profitable if the strike price were closer to the then stock price of $606, such as $590. It would have cost more, but delta would have been higher too. Indeed, in real life, I would have chosen a put option with a strike closer to the current stock price than the one used in the example.

Simple Long Put Risk and Reward Summary
Maximum profit: Limited to the strike price minus costs, as the lowest that a stock's price can go is zero. It occurs when the stock price is below strike price minus costs.
Maximum loss: limited to option premium paid plus costs.
Waiting for option premium to drop before buying an option will greatly improve the chances of making a profit.

---

iii. Simple Short Call

A simple short call refers to a strategy in which the investor intends to make money from selling a call option, while not owning the shares of the underlying stock. This is also called naked short call. If you recall from its payoff graph, a short call position has limited gain and unlimited loss. It would seem, then, only fools would sell options. However, in reality, a large proportion of profitable option trades come from selling options, since most options expire worthless.

While selling an option yields a limited gain, which is the option premium that the seller will receive at the beginning of the trade, there is one important factor that is in option seller/writer's favor: the passage of time. As time passes, the value of an option goes down due to time decay. An option seller can exit a position by buying back the option, and if she can do so when the option value has dropped, then the trade can be profitable.

The best time to sell a call option is when volatility is high, the underlying stock has gained a lot recently and is likely to experience a correction in the short term. This is the time when option value would be relatively high and has a fair chance of going lower.

Selling a call option can be seen as holding a bearish position on the underlying stock. If the stock price goes down, the call option will lose value, and the option seller can exit the position by buying back the option at a lower price than what he/she received. If the stock price goes up instead, the call option will go up in value. The call option seller will suffer a loss when the option value increases more than the premium that he/she received upon selling the option.

When you do not own shares that underlie the call option (naked short call), then either your broker will let you use margin, or not let you sell the call option at all. If you use margin, it means that you are only putting in a small proportion of the value of the underlying shares as collateral. If your bet is correct, your return is magnified. If the market goes against you and the stock price goes up instead, you would either have to supply additional funds, or your position will be closed involuntarily, even if the option is not yet in the money and the option buyer has not exercised the option, because margin is calculated on a daily basis. Margin management is an important part of naked short call strategy. Review the section on margin in the last chapter if you are not sure how margin is calculated, and make sure you have an optimal cash buffer to meet margin call at all time.

Let us look at an example of a naked short call. Say in October 2011, you came to the view that Apple Inc. will not be able to sustain its product design and marketing flairs after the demise of its chief executive, Steve Jobs. So you look up the call options of Apple Inc. as of 11 October 2011, when AAPL closed at $400.29, having gained 2.95% that day. For call options that would expire on 20 Jan 2012, you saw the following option prices (on the third column from the left).

390.00	AAPL120121C00390000	38.00	0.00	N/A	N/A	957	22,734
395.00	AAPL120121C00395000	36.05	0.00	N/A	N/A	432	5,344
400.00	AAPL120121C00400000	32.60	0.00	N/A	N/A	2,797	47,423
405.00	AAPL120121C00405000	30.20	0.00	N/A	N/A	399	4,538
410.00	AAPL120121C00410000	27.30	0.00	N/A	N/A	817	10,099
415.00	AAPL120121C00415000	25.40	0.00	N/A	N/A	135	3,620
420.00	AAPL120121C00420000	23.45	0.00	N/A	N/A	1,274	22,373
425.00	AAPL120121C00425000	21.00	0.00	N/A	N/A	329	6,992
430.00	AAPL120121C00430000	19.20	0.00	N/A	N/A	737	9,558
435.00	AAPL120121C00435000	17.90	0.00	N/A	N/A	124	2,699
440.00	AAPL120121C00440000	15.70	0.00	N/A	N/A	1,189	23,141
445.00	AAPL120121C00445000	14.28	0.00	N/A	N/A	210	2,353
450.00	AAPL120121C00450000	12.90	0.00	N/A	N/A	2,300	14,560
455.00	AAPL120121C00455000	11.95	0.00	N/A	N/A	60	1,432
460.00	AAPL120121C00460000	10.54	0.00	N/A	N/A	291	4,219

Source: Yahoo! Finance

You are confident that, by January 2012, AAPL's share price would not be able to gain by more than 15%, or exceed $460. So you sold one contract with strike at $460 and received $10.54 times 100 shares, i.e. $1,054.

The best outcome for you is if AAPL's share price stays below $460 on expiration. Even if the share price goes to $470, you will not suffer any loss, since the premium you received was $10.54.

If the share price goes to $500, then your payoff from the option would be -$40 per share. Part of this loss is offset by the premium received, so the actual loss per share would be $40-$10.54 = $29.46, and $2,946 per contract.

Exercise

An option writer does not have the right to exercise the option. Whenever the call option is in the money, which is when the stock price is above the strike price, there is a possibility that an option is exercised by the option holder, although the likelihood is low when the option still has time value. When that happens, the option writer has to deliver the underlying shares. Naked short call writers do not have the underlying shares, so they would have to borrow the shares from the broker and acquire a short position in the stock.

Expiration

Upon expiration, if a call option is in the money, most, if not all, of the option writers would be assigned to deliver the underlying shares. Again, naked short call writers will have to end up with a short position in the underlying stock.

Most option writers would like to see their options expire worthless, so that they can keep all the premium. To increase the chances of the options expiring worthless, naked call option writers would choose to sell options with short expiration, such as one month, so that time decay could eat away the option value.

Strike price

Call options with a lower strike price will have a higher premium than one with a higher strike price. At the same time, the risk of such options being in the money is also higher. Since potential loss from writing an option is unlimited, it would be wise to err on the safe side and build a decent safety margin into the strike price. One way to determine the size of the safety margin is to look at the recent movement of the stock price. If recently the weekly range of stock price movement is +/- $10, the strike price for a call option expiring within a month could be two times this value above the current stock price. If there is earnings announcement or other special event before the option expires, then the strike price should be even further from the current stock price.

Simple Short Call Risk and Reward Summary
Maximum profit: limited to option premium received minus costs. It occurs when stock price stays below the strike price on expiration of the option.
Maximum loss: unlimited, as the stock price goes higher. It occurs when the stock price is greater than strike price plus costs.
High volatility in underlying stock before the sale of the option will increase option premium and the chances of making a profit.

iv. Covered Call

A covered call refers to the selling of a call option when you have in possession the underlying stocks. This is a tactic usually used to generate income, since you will receive the option premium when you sell an option. The selling of a call option is combined with the ownership of the underlying shares for the purpose of liquidity protection. If a buyer of the option exercise his right to exchange the option for shares and your option is assigned, then your shares can be used to meet your obligation, i.e. the shares will be called away. Because of the ownership of the underlying shares, there is no need for your broker to worry about your ability to meet the option obligation, therefore you will not be forced to exit the position even when the position is losing money, and margin requirement will not be imposed. (Some people may disagree with my use of the term 'liquidity protection' here. My point is, even if you have other assets in your brokerage account, your broker may still not accept them as collateral for uncovered call options. If you do not have any asset that could be used to back up your short call position, then, indeed, it is not a liquidity problem, but a capital shortfall.)

For some investors, selling covered call options is the only way that they can sell call options, as some brokers do not allow inexperienced options traders to sell call options not backed by underlying shares.

Many investment books say that selling covered options is 'safe'. This could mislead some readers into thinking that selling call options does not involve risk, or a chance of losing money. That is not correct. If the stock price rises a lot above the strike price of the call option on expiration, then the option buyer could pay the seller just the strike price to gain possession of the underlying stocks which are now worth much more in the market. The premium collected from selling the call option may not be sufficient to cover the losses in such a scenario. The option writer will lose the potential profit from the long stock position that she would have made if she had not written the option.

There are two ways to sell covered call options. If selling covered options is used as a way to generate income repeatedly, then we are talking about selling options at far OTM strike prices, so that the chances of the call option being ITM is lower than that for OTM options with lower strike prices. Since the premium would be low, you would have to sell the covered calls for the same underlying stocks several times a year to make the strategy worthwhile. The more volatile is the stock price movement, the farther the options' strike price needs to be OTM.

The other way to sell covered call is to profit from stocks that have reached a price that suggests a peak is near. In such circumstances, you do not mind losing the stocks when the stock price reaches the strike price and the call options that you sold are called. You can earn higher premium per trade, because you would sell the call options at a strike price that is not too far above the current stock price. If you think your stock price has already reached a peak though, and is likely to experience large decline and unlikely to recover soon, it may be better to sell the stock now instead of holding on to the shares just to earn the call option premium, which could be very small compared to the loss from a collapse in stock price.

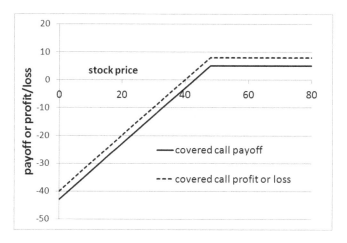

The above diagram shows the payoff and profit/loss of a covered call option. It has combined the payoff and profit or loss of a short call with those of a long stock position. The option premium received was $3 per share, while the underlying shares were bought at $43. The strike price was $48.

Let us use the shares of McDonald (MCD) to demonstrate the selling of covered call options with a view to generate income on a continuous basis. Suppose you own shares of MCD and you do not think the share price will go anywhere within the next two years. MCD is a relatively mature large cap stock, so its stock price is usually not as volatile as that of a small cap stock. The call option's strike price thus does not have to be too far above the current price for the same time frame as compared to the strike price for a smaller or less established company. It has a small dividend yield of around 2.5%, so we will ignore it for now.

On 26 July 2011, the shares of MCD closed at $88.02. For options with strike price at $92.50, we obtained the following quotes from Yahoo Finance:

Expiration date	Calendar Days to expiration	Premium quoted $	premium per day $
16 September 2011	52	0.35	0.006731
16 December 2011	123	1.41	0.011463
20 January 2012	158	1.67	0.01057
16 March 2012	213	2.25	0.010563
18 January 2013	420	5.00	0.011905

There was no option available with expiration date between March 2012 and January 2013 at that point in time. The options exchange will make them available only six to nine months ahead if there is sufficient demand, unless they are LEAPS.

On a per day basis, it seems that selling the January 2013 options would be most profitable. So if we sell the call options and they are not exercised, then by January 2013 our income would be $5, a total return of 4.9%, or annual return of 4.3%. If the stock price reached $97.5 ($92.5+$5) at option expiration, however, all gains from collecting option premiums would be gone, and any higher price on that expiration date would incur losses. For investors who had bought shares of MCD at a lower price earlier, do not want to trade often, and are satisfied with this level of income, selling this long-dated option would be a good idea.

For more active investors who can monitor the market more frequently and are willing to trade more in exchange for potentially higher income, on the other hand, we can trade options with shorter expiration. On 19 October 2011, MCD closed at $89.62. Its call options expiring on 20 January 2012 were last traded at the following prices:

70.00	MCD120121C00070000	**19.89**	0.00	19.75	19.90	51	4,533
72.50	MCD120121C00072500	**18.21**	↑0.73	17.35	17.50	1	1,149
75.00	MCD120121C00075000	**14.90**	↓0.05	15.00	15.10	22	7,176
77.50	MCD120121C00077500	**13.20**	↑0.80	12.65	12.80	1	1,518
80.00	MCD120121C00080000	**11.20**	↑0.85	10.45	10.55	33	11,285
82.50	MCD120121C00082500	**8.95**	↑1.08	8.35	8.45	5	3,407
85.00	MCD120121C00085000	**7.00**	↑0.70	6.40	6.50	684	9,675
87.50	MCD120121C00087500	**4.80**	↑0.80	4.65	4.75	18	4,059
90.00	MCD120121C00090000	**3.20**	0.00	3.20	3.30	107	9,782
92.50	MCD120121C00092500	**2.04**	↑0.06	2.04	2.10	103	3,667
95.00	MCD120121C00095000	**1.20**	↑0.14	1.19	1.23	85	5,818
97.50	MCD120121C00097500	**0.66**	↑0.09	0.63	0.66	51	1,654
100.00	MCD120121C00100000	**0.29**	↑0.06	0.30	0.33	53	1,741

Source: Yahoo! Finance

The option premium for the call option at strike $92.50 has gone up to $2.04, from $1.67 in July 2011. Since there would be 93 days to expiration from 19 October 2011, the premium per day is $0.021935.

Assume in July 2011 we sold the September $92.50 call option for $0.35, and then in October 2011 we sold the January 2012 $92.50 call option for $2.04. Assuming also that the strike price was not breached from July 2011 to January 2012, the two call options would give us $2.39 in this six month period, which can be translated into an annual return of 5.4%, if we had bought the stocks at the price of $88.02 in July 2011. This represents a slightly higher gain than from selling the longer dated options described earlier. We can make even more gain if we time the selling of options to periods of higher volatility, such as around earnings announcement.

If the stock price had gone up and the underlying shares were called away upon expiration on 20 January 2012, then your shares can book a capital gain of ($92.50 - $88.02=) $4.48. If the stock price reached much higher than the strike price on expiration, say, $100, you would suffer an opportunity loss of $7.50 ($100 - $92.50) per share, which can be offset by the premium collected ($2.39) and the capital gain of $4.48.

If a covered call option is exercised when the stock price is peaking, this is of course a good thing. It means that the stock you held is sold just before the price starts to fall. On the other hand, if the stock price continues to rise after your covered call option is exercised, you may be able to recoup the loss from selling your shares at a low price by doing what else but repeating the same act again? You should buy back the shares quickly and sell covered call options. When the stock price goes higher quickly, the higher volatility will drive the option price higher. If the higher option price can more than offset the loss from selling the stock at a lower price than the market commands, then you will still make a profit. In other words, you do not have to sit there and sulk when one option trade turns against you. You can turn the table provided you think ahead and can act fast.

If you buy the underlying stock at the same time that you sell the call options, the strategy is called "buy-write". It is a strategy that is very welcomed by the options brokers, since they can earn commissions on both transactions. To me, the buy-write strategy only makes sense in a small number of cases, one is if your broker does not allow you to sell call options without underlying shares to cover, but you have spotted a very attractive price for a short option position.

One final point: if you buy 100 shares of a stock and sell a call option of the stock (covered call writing) at a strike price that equals the price of the shares that you bought, the payoff graph would be similar to a short put position of the same strike price. The diagram below shows the payoff of a stock bought at $40 and a short call with strike at $40. We will discuss the differences of the two strategies after we explain the short put strategy in the next section.

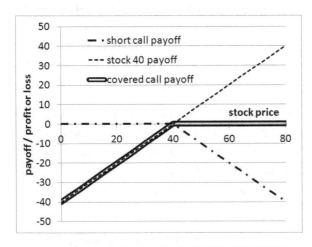

Covered Call Risk and Reward Summary
Maximum profit: limited to option premium received plus the difference between the purchase price of the underlying stocks and strike price as long as

the purchase price is below the strike price, minus costs.

Maximum loss: up to the strike price of the call option minus the option premiums received. It occurs when the underlying stock price goes to zero. Loss is incurred when the stock price is less than the strike price minus option premium received minus the gain between the purchase price and the strike price.

The long stock position removes the liquidity risk when the short call is in the money.

v. Simple Short Put

An investor will engage in a simple short put option trade if he/she wants to profit from a drop in the value of a put option. The maximum that he/she can collect is the premium that he/she gets when he/she first sold the option. If the option value goes higher when you need to close the position, then you would lose money in the trade, and theoretically there is no limit to the potential loss.

Since a put option usually goes up in value when the stock price goes down, seller/write of a simple put option would want to see the opposite happens, i.e. the stock price goes up or at least stays above the strike price during the life of the option.

Say, in October 2011, you believed that the worst was over for Bank of America (BAC), whose share price closed at $6.37 on 11 October 2011, as compared to $14 at the beginning of 2011.

Put Options							Expire at close Friday, May 18, 2012
Strike	Symbol	Last	Chg	Bid	Ask	Vol	Open Int
2.00	BAC120519P00002000	0.20	0.00	N/A	N/A	165	3,742
3.00	BAC120519P00003000	0.35	0.00	N/A	N/A	660	10,024
4.00	BAC120519P00004000	0.58	0.00	N/A	N/A	6,589	14,484
5.00	BAC120519P00005000	0.87	0.00	N/A	N/A	228	22,109
6.00	BAC120519P00006000	1.30	0.00	N/A	N/A	151	33,853
7.00	BAC120519P00007000	1.75	0.00	N/A	N/A	74	28,188
8.00	BAC120519P00008000	2.41	0.00	N/A	N/A	20	20,203
9.00	BAC120519P00009000	3.06	0.00	N/A	N/A	6	34,362
10.00	BAC120519P00010000	3.95	0.00	N/A	N/A	195	9,268
11.00	BAC120519P00011000	4.80	0.00	N/A	N/A	326	1,321
12.00	BAC120519P00012000	5.76	0.00	N/A	N/A	10	2,798
13.00	BAC120519P00013000	6.75	0.00	N/A	N/A	2	772
14.00	BAC120519P00014000	7.85	0.00	N/A	N/A	17	3,448
15.00	BAC120519P00015000	8.85	0.00	N/A	N/A	25	501

Source: Yahoo! Finance

If you think that by May 2012, BAC will very unlikely go down to below $5, you can sell the $5 put option for around $0.87. For each contract, you will receive $87. Since the stock was at $6.37 when you bought it, a $5 put option is an out of money (OTM) option, and all the option value is time value. As long as the option value does not fall by more than $0.87 per share below the strike price on expiration, you can make a profit. This means that your breakeven stock price at expiration is ($5-$0.87=) $4.13.

If you have a bullish opinion on a stock, why would you be bothered with a short put option, where the gain is limited and loss can be substantial? When volatility is high, option price is high. You can sell the put option at a good price, while the call option could be expensive to buy. If volatility goes down after you sold an option, the option value will go down, giving you an opportunity to profit, even if the stock price does not move much.

Selling an option also gives you cash up front. If your broker has a very low margin requirement for initiating and maintaining a short put option position, and you are short on cash, then selling an option could be more viable for you than buying a call option, but you have to monitor your position closely to manage your risk.

In addition, selling (or writing) a put option is a good way to acquire stocks at a low price, particularly stocks that are volatile. Say you like the stock of Qualcomm (QCOM), a designer of computer chips. It is currently trading at $56.50. You would like to buy some shares but think that the market could drag the stock price down a little in the near future, before it recovers. You could then write a put option with a strike price near your target purchase price, say $50, with an expiration that will likely see the stock price bottoming, say five months from now. In November 2011, that option was valued at $2.60. This means that, if the stock price falls below $50 at any time, your option could be exercised by the option buyer, and you would have to pay $50 to buy the stocks. Since you received $2.60 upfront from writing the option, you will only incur losses if the stock price falls below $47.40. However, since you were prepared to buy the stock at $50 any way, you are no worse off than if you had bought the stocks directly.

Since a short put position can incur a large loss, the maximum value of which happens when the stock price goes to zero, and your broker would be on the hook if you cannot meet the obligation, your broker will not let you open a short put position without some protection. If your broker is aggressive, he will let you use margin. If he is conservative, he will set aside an amount of cash that is equivalent to a large loss of the option in your account (cash secured short put). With a margin account, margin is calculated on a daily basis, so when the option value goes up substantially one day, and you do not have enough cash in the account to meet margin call, your position will be closed by the broker, denying your option of any chance of recovery. If the put option is exercised, and you do not have sufficient funds to buy the underlying shares, your broker could sell your other positions to pay for it. These are risks that an option writer has to manage.

Since the payoff graph of a short put option is the same as that for a covered call with the same strike price and premium, how does a covered call position compare with a short put position?

Most of the time, the two strategies are used for different purposes. As explained before, covered call is used mainly to either generate income or to generate income and sell the stock at a slightly higher price when an investor already owns the underlying stocks. The investor's view is mainly bearish. A short put, on the other hand, is used mainly to express a flat to bullish view on the stock price. In my view, option strategies that include a stock position should not be viewed together with those that do not, as the stock position usually serves other purposes, such as a remnant of a bullish view in the past, or to meet the liquidity need for option trading.

Some people would point to the "downside" protection properties of the two strategies and suggest that the two strategies are interchangeable for this purpose, since their payoff graphs are the same. When the stock price drops, a short put has positive payoff as long as the drop does not exceed the amount of the premium received. The short call in the covered call can offset the loss experienced by the long stock position up to the value of the premium received. But a simple short put has a different payoff graph from that of a protective put, as can be seen in the next section. Thus, it does not serve much purpose to compare covered call with a simple short put when downside protection of an existing long stock position is being considered.

Compared with buying the shares of a stock, selling put options can be used when you do not know whether the stock price will rise: you only need to be quite sure that it will not fall any further.

Short Put Risk and Reward Summary
Maximum profit: limited to the option premium received.

Maximum loss: the full value of the strike price minus premium received as the stock price drops towards zero. Loss is incurred when the stock price is below strike price minus premium received.

High volatility in underlying stock before the sale of the option will increase option premium and the chances of making a profit.

---

vi. Protective Put

A protective put is to buy a put option for stocks that you already own, so that, if the stock price declines, your loss from the decline in stock value would be offset by the gain from the put option, which goes up in value when the stock price goes down. A protective put is thus a defensive move that costs money, not an income generating tactic.

The payoff graph for a protective put is similar to that of a simple long call. When we combine the long stock position with the long put, we add the payoff of each vertically on the payoff graph. The long stock payoff is a line that intersects at 45 degree (assuming the same scale is used on both axes) the x-axis representing zero payoff at the stock price that protection is deemed necessary, which is usually assumed to be the current stock price. The strike price of the associating put option is also normally set at that price.

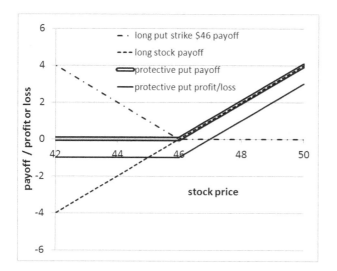

That such a tactic exists does not tell us whether we should use it, and if so, when we should use it. Unlike the situation when we consider whether to buy life insurance, in stock investing, we can choose to terminate the underlying risk. If we are worried that the price of a stock could go down a lot, we can choose either to sell the stock, or buy a protective put option.

The advantage of using a protective put instead of selling the stock is that, in case you are wrong, i.e. the stock price did not go down, the most you would lose is the option price you paid to purchase it. Whereas if you had sold the stocks and then the stock price goes up a lot, your lost profit could be very high. So a protective put limits your lost profit. Another advantage of using a protective put is if the stock price goes down first and then goes back up, you would not miss the opportunity to buy back the stock after having sold it earlier.

If you are right, though, and the stock price does go down, buying a protective put costs more than if you had simply sold the stock before the price went down. If you want lock-step protection of stock price decline, the put options that you buy will either have to be deep in the money, or at the money and near expiration. Either one would not be cheap.

The consideration is therefore which outcome is more undesirable to you, and how likely is that outcome. In my opinion, investors who have made some profit and are worried about losses would be better off selling the stocks instead of buying protective puts. Investors who are very confident about the future of their stock will of course not consider protective put or any of its alternatives.

Let us use Apple, Inc. (AAPL) again as an example. Suppose, after Steve Jobs' death, you are still confident that the company will continue to do well in future, but you are mindful that in the short term, the company might experience some difficulties. You would like to hold on to your AAPL shares but hate to sustain losses if the share price does go down in the interim.

On 19 October 2011, AAPL closed at $398.62. Its put options expiring on 16 December 2011 were trading at these prices:

370.00	AAPL111217P00370000	10.30
375.00	AAPL111217P00375000	11.80
380.00	AAPL111217P00380000	13.50
385.00	AAPL111217P00385000	15.30
390.00	AAPL111217P00390000	17.35
395.00	AAPL111217P00395000	19.27
400.00	AAPL111217P00400000	21.95
405.00	AAPL111217P00405000	24.64
410.00	AAPL111217P00410000	27.45
415.00	AAPL111217P00415000	29.90
420.00	AAPL111217P00420000	33.10
425.00	AAPL111217P00425000	36.80
430.00	AAPL111217P00430000	40.00

Source: Yahoo! Finance

Since the stock price at the time these prices were determined was at $398.62, the put options with strike price at $400 have an intrinsic value of $1.38 and a time value of ($21.95-$1.38) $20.57. The options with strike at $370 are OTM, so all their values ($10.30) are time value.

If you had bought your AAPL shares at $380, which put option should you buy for protection if you hold the option to expiration? For the put option with strike at $400, the breakeven stock price is ($400-$21.95=) $378.05. The one with strike at

74

$370 has breakeven at $359.70. The higher strike put option will therefore provide protection earlier, but the stock price still has to drop more than 5% from $400 for it to be worthwhile.

Protective Put Risk and Reward Summary
Maximum profit: Unlimited. Equivalent to the gain in stock price minus option premium paid.
Maximum loss: Option premium paid plus costs.

This is a worthwhile strategy only when the price of the put option is very low.

---

vii. Bull spreads

The four basic option types can be mixed and matched to create many more strategies. A spread generally involves buying one option and simultaneously selling another option of the same type, i.e. both are call options or both are put options for the same underlying stocks. If the two options have the same expiration date, then the pair is called a vertical spread. If they have different expiration dates, then the pair is either a calendar spread or diagonal spread.

Bull spread is a strategy for investors who want to profit from a rise in stock price using two options. One of the two options is used to achieve the main objective of the strategy (to gain from rising stock price) while the other option serves another purpose, either to reduce the cost of implementing the strategy or reduce its risk. Another advantage of a bull spread is the neutralization of time decay - the time decay of a long position is compensated by the gain from time decay of a short position. Bull call spread involves two call options, while bull put spread involves two put options.

Let us start with bull call spread. It involves the investor buying a call option at a strike that is at or slightly above the current stock price, and selling a call option at a higher strike price to offset the cost of the first option. In exchange for such reduced cost, the investor has to accept limited gain even if the stock price goes much higher than the strike price of the second call option. In fact, the maximum gain that the investor can get from a bull call spread is the difference between the two strike prices, before option premiums and commissions. Say the lower strike price for the long call is labeled strike L and the higher strike price for the short call is labeled strike H. The current stock price is the spot price. The payoff equation can be worked out as such:

Long Call option payoff = max(spot - strike L, 0)

Short Call option payoff = -max(spot- strike H, 0)

Long call option payoff + short call option payoff = max(spot - strike L, 0) - max(spot - strike H, 0)

If strike H > spot > strike L, then total payoff = spot - strike L

If spot > strike H > strike L, then total payoff = spot - strike L - spot + strike H = strike H - strike L

If strike H > strike L > spot, then total payoff = 0

In other words, a bull call spread will have a limited upside and limited downside. It reaches its maximum payoff when the current stock price equals the higher strike price. The payoff remains the same even if the current stock price goes higher. Its minimum payoff is zero.

For example, if you buy a call option with strike price of $38 for $4 and sell a call option with strike price of $46 for $3, its payoff and profit or loss graphs would look like this:

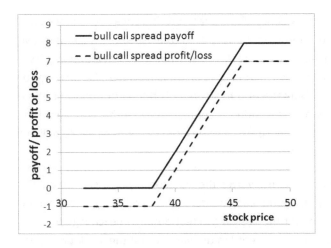

At all times, the payoff and the profit or loss graphs differ by $1, because you paid $4 for the call option and received $3 from selling the other call option at a higher strike price. (If you have a net outlay in initiating a trade, such as this one, that trade is called a debit trade. If you receive money when initiating a trade, then it is called a credit trade.)

How will the value of a bull call spread actually behave? We can get some idea from examining the delta of a bull call spread like the one in the graph above that has, for example, 30 days to expire, based on assumptions of risk free rate of 3% and volatility of 40%:

Stock price	$36	$38	$40	$42	$44	$46	$48
Long call strike $38	0.347	0.531	0.701	0.829	0.913	0.959	0.983
Short call strike $46	-0.02	-0.056	-0.127	-0.237	-0.379	-0.531	-0.674
Bull Call Spread	0.327	0.475	0.574	0.592	0.534	0.428	0.309

You will notice from the table above which uses the Black-Scholes model (a popular options model) that, the bull call spread is most sensitive to movement of the underlying stock price when it is midway between the two strike prices. Therefore, do not feel too frustrated when the value of your bull call spread does not seem to go up much when the stock price is moving up from near the lower strike price level.

Put another way, the sweet spot for a bull spread is when the stock price is near the mid-point of the two strike prices, and the options are approaching expiration. If you recall from the delta graphs in the previous chapter, delta will move higher for call options that are ITM (the long call position of the bull spread), and lower for those that are OTM when they have very little time left until expiration (the short call of the spread). That is the time when a small increase in stock price will translate into a big change in the bull call spread's value.

Bull Call Spread Risk and Reward Summary

Maximum profit: When stock price reaches the (higher) strike price of the OTM short call option. It is limited to the difference of the two strike prices minus the net premium paid.

Maximum loss: Limited to the net option premium paid plus costs. It occurs when the stock price is at or less than the strike price of the long call option.

A variation of the bull call spread is bull call ratio spread. Instead of buying one call option and selling another call option, a bull call ratio spread involves selling more than one call option for every call option purchased. For example, if, instead of selling one call option with strike at $46 for $3 in the above bull call spread, we sell two call options with strike at $50 for $2.50 each. As in the bull call spread, we still buy a call option at strike $38. The payoff and profit/loss graphs will look like this:

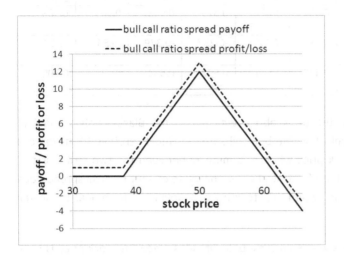

Since we sold two call options for $2.50 each, and bought one call option for $4, we actually net $1 from the premiums (a credit trade).

The payoff equation for the ratio spread is:

Long call option payoff + N x short call option payoff = max(spot - strike L, 0) - N * max(spot - strike H, 0)

with N being the number of short call options with strike H.

From the payoff graph, you can see that the ratio spread has positive payoff when the stock price is between the lower strike price and the lower strike price plus two times the difference between the higher and lower strike prices (strike L + N x (strike H - strike L)). For our example, this means the spread has positive payoff between $38 and (2 x (50-38) =) $62.

That is the good news. The bad news is, if the stock price goes beyond $62, then the loss can be as high as the stock price can go, minus $62 (excluding the premiums), and is unlimited in theory.

Does this mean that the ratio spread is more risky than the straight bull call spread? Looking at the payoff graphs alone, it would seem so. However, if we use a higher strike price for the short call positions in the ratio spread, as we did in the example, then we are reducing the chances that the spread will incur a loss.

An examination of the delta position of the ratio spread, though, does remind us to be cautious in using ratio spread, as delta is higher when the payoff is on the way down (i.e. when stock price is over $50) than when it is on the way up (when the stock price is between $38 and $50). This means that, when the price of the underlying stock starts to move above the higher strike price of the ratio spread, the payoff can deteriorate rapidly.

stock price	38	42	46	50	54	58	62
long call	0.531	0.8293	0.959	0.993	0.999	0.999	1
2 short call	0.021	0.149	0.517	1.063	1.547	1.830	1.949
ratio spread total delta	0.511	0.680	0.443	-0.070	-0.548	-0.830	-0.949

> **Bull Call Ratio Spread Risk and Reward Summary**
> **Maximum profit**: occurs when the stock price is at the strike price of the short call options. It is limited by the amount calculated in this equation:
> [option premium collected from selling options+((difference in strike prices)-option premium paid for each long call position) times the number of call options bought]
> **Maximum loss**: Unlimited, if stock price rises above the sum of the long call strike and the number of call options sold times the difference in strike prices (that is, when stock price >[strike L + N x (strike H - strike L)]).

Let us now look at the other type of bull spread: the bull put spread. It consists of one short put option at a strike price that is near the current stock price, and one long option with a higher strike price. The first option, a short put option, allows the investor to collect the option premium. Part of this money can be used to pay for the second option, which is cheaper because the strike price is higher. The remaining amount is the net premium collected.

If the price of the underlying stock goes up or stays flat after the trade is initiated, then the investor can keep all the net premium collected upon expiration of the options.

The second put option, a long put option with a higher strike price, offers a protection from unlimited losses in case the price of the underlying stock goes down instead of going up or staying flat. In sum, a bull put spread also has limited loss and limited gain. Its payoff graph has the same shape as that for a bull call spread.

Bull Put Spread Risk and Reward Summary
Maximum profit: When stock price equals or exceeds the (higher) strike price of the short put option. It is limited to the net premium received minus commissions.

Maximum loss: When stock price equals or less than the (lower) strike price of the long put option. It is limited to the difference in strike prices of the two options minus the net premium received minus commissions.

How do you choose between the two types of bull spreads? The bull call spread involves buying a call option at a lower strike and selling another call option at a higher strike. A bull put spread requires buying a put option at a lower strike and selling a put option at a higher strike. We would like to maximize the income and minimize the expenditure.

The main difference between the two types of bull spreads is the risk/reward profile. The bull call spread has maximum profit that equals the difference between the two strike prices, while that of the bull put spread is the net premium received. Their maximum loss is the opposite of these two values. We want to have higher reward and lower risk. We can predetermine the difference between the two strike prices, and compared the net premium received or paid, to see which spread is better at a particular point in time.

viii. Bear spreads

The opposite of a bull spread is a bear spread. Investors who want to make money from falling stock price can institute either a bear call spread or a bear put spread.

For a bear put spread, the investor will buy a put option with strike near the current stock price, so that it will gain from falling stock price, and sell a put option with a strike a bit lower than the current stock price in order to use the premium collected to reduce the cash outlay required by the first option. The investor expects only a small fall in stock price if he/she uses this strategy.

Long Put option payoff = max(strike H - spot, 0)
Short Put option payoff = - max(strike L - spot, 0)
Long put option payoff + short put option payoff = max(strike H - spot, 0) - max(strike L - spot, 0)

If strike H > spot > strike L, then total payoff = strike H - spot
If spot > strike H > strike L, then total payoff = 0
If strike H > strike L > spot, then total payoff = strike H - spot - strike L + spot = strike H - strike L

In other words, a bear put spread will have a limited upside and limited downside. It reaches its maximum payoff, which equals strike H - strike L, when the stock price equals the lower strike price. If the spot price goes below the lower strike price, the payoff of the spread will still be strike H - strike L.

A bear put spread is a debit spread because the premium of a put option with a higher strike price is always higher than that of a put option with a lower strike price. A bear put spread investor will have to pay more to buy the put option with a higher strike price, while receiving less when selling the put option with a lower strike price. Shown below are the payoff and profit /loss graphs of a bear put spread that is made up of a long put option with strike at $46 bought for $4 and a short put option with strike at $38 sold for $3:

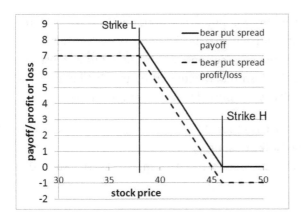

As can be seen from the graphs, the maximum payoff from this bear put spread is ($46 - $38) $8, and after netting the premiums, the maximum profit is $7, which will occur if the stock price goes down to $38 or less.

Bear Put Spread Risk and Reward Summary
Maximum profit occurs when the stock price is at or less than the strike price of the short put option. It is limited to the difference of the two strike prices minus the net premium paid.
Maximum loss happens when the stock price is at or more than the strike price of the long put option. It is limited to the net premium paid.

Below I show the payoff and profit / loss graphs of a bear put ratio spread that involves buying one put (at strike H = $46) and selling two puts at strike L ($38) and for premiums that are same as the bear put spread described above:

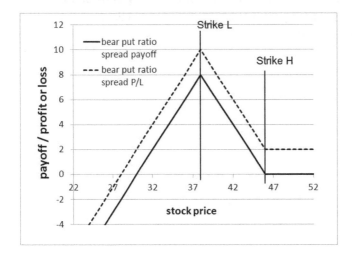

With two short put options, the profit profile of the spread is improved. If the investor receives a net payment on initiating the trade, then the spread is a credit spread. The tradeoff of this is that, if the stock price goes below the lower strike of $38, profit will be first reduced, and then losses will start to grow after the stock price falls below $28. You can check if this is correct by using the payoff and profit/loss formulae.

The payoff formula : N1 x max (strike H - spot, 0) - N2 x max (strike L - spot, 0)
The profit / loss formula = payoff - net premiums paid
If spot < strike L, payoff = N1 x (strike H - spot) - N2 x (strike L - spot)

N1 being the number of long puts, and N2 is the number of short puts. Since this is a credit spread, the net premiums paid is negative, so the amount should be added to the payoff value to arrive at the P/L value. As can be seen from the P/L graph, the spread has two breakeven points. At a breakeven, P/L = 0. At the lower breakeven point, spot = 2 x strike L - strike H - net premiums paid. If we put the strike prices and the net premium paid into the formula, we can find the lower breakeven price.

Bear Put Ratio Spread Risk Reward Summary
Maximum Profit occurs when the underlying stock price is at the lower strike price (that of the short put option position). It is limited to the product of the number of long put options and the difference in strike prices minus the net premium paid (or plus net premium received).

Maximum Loss. Losses start to occur when the underlying stock price falls below this value:
[N1 x (strike H - PremH) - N2 x (strike L - PremL)]/ (N1 - N2)
Where PremH is the premium paid for each long put, and PremL is the premium received for each short put. Maximum loss occurs when stock price falls to zero, which is equal to this value:
N1 x (strike H - PremH) - N2 x (strike L - PremL)

Both bear put spread and bear ratio put spread are appropriate only when the expected downward move of the underlying stock price is small, with the latter spread being more risky but cheaper to initiate.

There is another kind of spread that can be used in situations where the investor expects a large decline in the price of a stock.

ix. Put backspread (reverse put ratio spread)

A put backspread involves selling a put option at near current stock price, and buying a bigger number of put options at a lower strike price. Since overall the spread has a net long put position (more long puts than short puts), it is a strategy that is used to express a highly bearish view on a stock. Take a look at the payoff and P/L graphs below and you will see how it can be used.

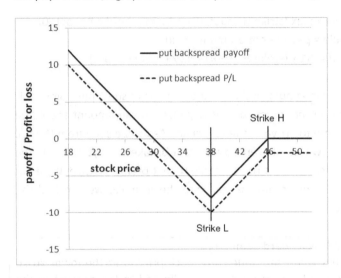

Below: A simple put option with strike at Strike L.

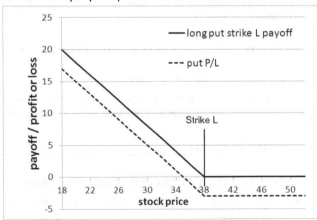

Shown below the diagram for the backspread is diagram for a simple put option. The simple put option has the same strike price ($38) as the two long puts position in the backspread trade, and the same premium of $3 each. The put backspread has a short put position, which yields the investor $4. As a result the backspread has a net premium cost of $2, while the simple put option costs $3. This would appear to be the only advantage of using a put backspread instead of a simple put when an investor wants to profit from a declining stock price. Indeed, for stock prices around strike L, the spread loses money. Also notice that, because of the dip of the payoff around strike L, the simple put is more profitable than the backspread at prices below strike L.

If we are going to use a put backspread instead of a simple put, we would need to use one that gives us more advantages. How about one that has three long put options instead of two?

Box 5   Visualizing strategies with multiple options

While single options can be understood quite readily, it could be a challenge to get one's head around a spread that involves more than two options. The payoff and profit/loss graphs are indispensable aids in explaining these complex strategies, and investors should be able to construct such graphs from graphs of the four basic options strategies.

Some rules can help:

- Add the payoff and profit/loss of multiple options **vertically** in a graph to get the payoff and profit/loss position of the strategy at various stock prices.
- Identify the range(s) of stock prices that each option is ITM. At each range, net out the position to obtain the slope of the payoff (or profit/loss) for the strategy.
- if there is more than one option of the same type (e.g. several long put options, or all short put options etc.), then the slope will be steeper from the strike price where the options start to overlap. But the slope cannot be more than 90 degree steep.

For example, let us look at a spread with two long puts at strike H and three short puts at strike L, strike H being a higher strike price than strike L.

What would the payoff graph of the spread look like? Long puts will have a slope up from the strike to the top left side of a graph, while short puts will have a slope down from the strike to the bottom left of the graph. From stock price zero to strike L, all five options are ITM, including the short option positions, only that they have negative values, not positive values. Since two options are long and three options are short, the net effect is one short option, so the graph of a short

---

option position, which is a straight line going from strike L on the x-axis to south west with a slope of 1 down : 1 across, will apply. Its position on the y-axis at strike L, on the other hand, has to be found by looking at the section of the graph to its right.

Between strike L and strike H, only the two long puts are ITM. The payoff in this section is that of two long puts, which is a straight line sloping from strike H on the x-axis to the north west at a rate of 2 up : 1 across. The value of the y coordinate at strike L is obtained by multiplying the difference between strike H and strike L by two, the number of net option positions, plus the y coordinate value at the other end of this section of the payoff graph. If strike H is $20 and strike L is $14, then the y coordinate would be (2 × (20 − 14)) $12 higher than the y coordinate of the graph at strike H. In the graph below, strike L is $38 and strike H is $46. Can you figure out its y coordinate at strike H?

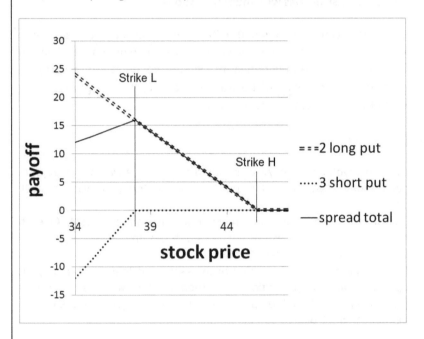

At stock prices greater than strike H, all five options are OTM, which means that the payoff graph is a horizontal line that runs along the x-axis with its y coordinate at zero.

If we visualize the put backspread with three long put options at strike L and one short put at strike H, we will be able to deduce two points without drawing the graph. First, from price zero to strike L, the slope of the net long put option positions would be steeper than that of the backspread before. For every one unit drop in stock price, the spread payoff would go up by two units. There will be no difference in the rest of the payoff graph, since, between strike L and strike H, only the short put position is ITM.

Second, the profit and loss graph would shift lower, by the premium paid for one additional long put.

In sum, even a put backspread with three long put and one short put at a higher strike will have advantage over a simple put only when the stock price goes very low. When we choose between a simple put and a put backspread, in my view only when the premium of the short put is much higher than the cost of one long put would a backspread make sense. It is an example of being simple is more beautiful.

To recap the last several option strategies that use put options, I have put them in a summary table:

	Low strike	High strike	Intention to profit from
Bull put spread	1 long OTM put	1 short ITM put	Small increase to stable price
Bear put spread	1 short OTM put	1 long ITM put	Small drop to stable price
Bear put ratio spread	2 short OTM put	1 long ITM put	Small drop to stable price
Put backspread	2 long put	1 short put	Large drop in share price

x.   Volatility bets using Straddles and strangles

One of the major characteristics of options trading that makes them attractive is that they allow money to be made on stock volatility. Option theories suggest that the price of an option, be it a call or put option, goes up when the stock price's volatility goes up, and actual option price movements suggest that this is true in most cases. (In theory, volatility can go up due to either a big price movement upward or a big movement down. In real life, a drop in price is likely to increase the value of implied volatility more than that caused by the same percentage increase in stock price.)

There are many ways to profit from changes in volatility. The purest way to do so, that is, with no bet on directional movement of the underlying stock price at all, is to buy a pair of call and put options for the same underlying stock at the same strike price for the same expiration date. This is called a straddle. The total cost of this trade would be the sum of the premiums for the pair of options. If the stock price goes up, the call option will gain in value, while the put option will lose value, but the loss is capped by the total premium value. Likewise, if the stock price goes down, the call option will lose value while the put option will gain value. As long as the underlying stock price makes moves sufficiently large in a short period of time so that the option value that goes up exceeds the total cost of the premiums, then the trade could be profitable. That's the theory, anyway.

Since the option value increase induced by stock price volatility has to be large enough to cover the cost of the two options, we need to look for two conditions before we initiate a straddle. One, the expected volatility increase should be large. Two, the premium prices that we are going to pay to purchase the options should be as low as possible.

If you observe that the price volatility of a stock is lower than usual a week or two after quarterly earnings announcement, or the stock market is quiet such as during the months of May and June, and you believe it will increase before the next earnings announcement or at year end, you could look for some cheap options during such times, with the purpose of selling them when volatility increases later.

Premium price is low when stock price volatility is low, and when the time to expiration is short. Therefore, you do not have much time, like no more than three months, to get the correct volatility movement.

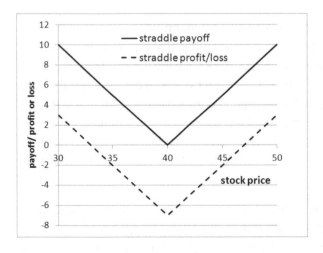

The above diagram shows the payoff and profit/loss graphs of a straddle with strike price of $40. The total premiums paid for the two options were $7. The breakeven prices are at +/- $7 of the strike price, which means that the stock price has to move at least $7 on either side of the strike price before the spread is profitable.

Why should both options have the same strike price? Presumably your view about directionless volatility is formed based on the current stock price. Thus your strike price, which is the same for both call and put option, should be at or near the current stock price.

When the put and call options have the same strike price, the absolute value of their theoretical delta will add up to 1. If the options are at the money, and they are close to expiration, for example, they will both have a absolute delta of 0.5, positive for a long call option, and negative for a long put option. If the stock price is such that the call option is in the money, then the put option will be out of money, and the absolute value of the call option's delta would be higher. If the stock price moves higher, then the effect of delta could make the call option's value go up more than the drop in the put option's value, allowing more profit to be made if the trade is to be settled before expiration. In other words, the straddle will become a directional trade if the underlying stock starts to make big moves in one direction. The total delta position will become positive if the underlying stock starts to go up, because the call option will have delta of more than 0.5 (e.g. 0.6), and the put option will have delta of more than -0.5 (e.g. -0.4). The total delta value (obtained by adding the two delta values) is 0.2, which is a slightly bullish bet.

If the price of the underlying stock starts to go down instead, the call option will have delta of less than 0.5 (e.g. 0.4), and the put option will have delta of less than -0.5 (e.g. -0.6). The total delta value is -0.2, a slightly bearish bet. Big volatility will likely exaggerate the difference and make the trade more profitable.

Straddle Risk and Reward Summary
Maximum profit occurs when the stock price is far away from the strike price. Theoretically it can be unlimited, if the stock price shoots to the moon, or limited to the strike price if the stock price falls to zero.
Maximum loss occurs if the stock price stays at the strike price, and equals the sum of the premiums paid, plus commissions.

Since the cost of a straddle is high relative to a single option trade, some people prefer to find ways to reduce the cost. One way is to buy the call option at a strike price slightly higher than the spot price, and the put option at a slightly lower strike price. This trade is called a Strangle. The premium prices of these options would be lower than at the money options. The trade off is that the payoff graph is now not a V shape, but a groove shape with a flat bottom. This means that there is a stock price range within which you will not get any payoff from the pair of options after incurring the cost of the option premiums.

Or, if you have a slightly stronger view in one direction than the other, then you could buy one option closer to the side of that direction, and the other option further from it. Once you move away from the same strike price, the option delta would stop complementing each other. The option with strike price farther from the current stock price will have a lower delta (in absolute value) than the option that is closer. If the stock price moves in the direction of the option that has a strike price closer to the original stock price, i.e. your bet, then that option's value will likely increase more than the drop in value of the other option. This would be in your favor. But if the stock price moves in the other direction, the gain in one option could be less than the loss in the other. This is a risk you have to bear in mind, in addition to the risk of the stock price falling between the two strike prices.

xi. Reverse iron butterfly

Another way to reduce the cost of a straddle is to sell options at strike price that are farther away from the current stock price than the strike prices of the call and put options, so that these additional options have very high chances of expiring worthless and allow the seller to keep all of the option premiums. For example, if the current stock price is at $40, you can buy a call option and a put option with strike at $40 (middle strike), then sell a put option with strike at $30 (low strike), and sell a call option with strike at $50 (high strike), all with the same expiration date. What does the payoff graph of this set of four options look like, if the premiums are $4, $3, $2.5 and $3.5 respectively?

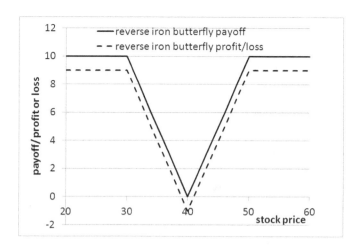

This is called a reverse iron butterfly. (You can check if this graph is correct by drawing the payoff graph of the four options independently, and then add up their values vertically to see if you will get this graph.) As can be seen from the graph, the breakeven prices (where profit/loss = 0) are much closer to the middle strike price than in the case of a straddle. This is an example of how some traders would use additional options to either reduce the cost of a trade or increase the premium collected from a basic option tactic. Many fancy options tactic names are the result of such layered tactics, e.g. condors are strangles plus another pair of call and put options in the other direction (if strangles are long positions, then the second pair of options would be short positions) and different strike prices.

Apart from this one, there are many types of butterfly spreads, such as long butterfly, short butterfly, modified butterfly, each with its own risk reward characteristics. They are called butterfly spreads because the shape of the payoff graph is like a butterfly, with a spike in the middle that looks like a butterfly's body when viewed in cross-section, and a wing on each side.

Just because a strategy is more complicated does not mean that it is a superior one. The cost of trading more options of different types is high, as each portion of the strategy is charged commission separately. A reverse iron butterfly involves four trades. The problem of bid/ask spread is compounded as well.

Reverse Iron Butterfly Risk and Reward Summary
Maximum profit is the difference between the high strike and the middle strike, minus the net premium paid. It occurs when the stock price is either higher than the highest strike price of the three, or lower than the lowest strike price.
Maximum loss is limited to total the cost of purchasing two options minus the

xii. Short Strangle

In the last section, we introduced the concept of using a pair of short options to reduce the cost of a straddle trade. We could actually use the pair of short options on their own as an income generating tactic. The best situation to use a pair of short options, one short call and one short put, is when you think that, after a volatile move in the stock price, it will settle within a range. The strike price of the short call should be the maximum price of the stock movement within the range, and the strike price of the short put the minimum price of the stock movement. This is called a short strangle, and if it works out, we will collect all the premiums from both short options. If it does not, however, a short strangle can incur large losses, and thus must be managed properly.

The first step in managing the downside risk of a short strangle, or any option trade, is to set it up carefully.

The first leg of the short strangle could be either the short put or the short call. Choose one after the target stock's price has moved too much in one direction and is more likely to go the other direction in the near future. If the stock price has dropped a lot, and is likely to have bottomed, sell an OTM put option that will give you a decent safety cushion. For example, if a stock's price has dropped 15%, and during its recent worst selloff the maximum price decline was 21%, you could double the difference of 6% and set the strike price at 12% below the current price. If the stock price has moved up too much, on the other hand, we should sell an OTM call option with strike price above the current stock price by a similar safety margin.

We would complete the setup by selling another option in the other direction. If we had sold a call option to take advantage of an overextended increase in stock price, for the second leg we would sell a put option at a strike price that is substantially below the current spot price. This safety margin is to be wider than that for the first option, because the stock price was seen as being overextended in the direction of the first option, so it could swing back to and beyond the perceived neutral position.

This second option serves three purposes. First, it will provide a limited hedge to the first short option position. Say the first leg is a short call. A short call is basically a bearish bet on the underlying stock's price, and it will lose money if the stock price goes up. A short put, on the other hand, is a bullish bet on the underlying stock's price, and will let the seller keep the option premium if the stock price goes up. Hence the short put will hedge the short call up to the value of the premium received from the short put. If the stock price goes down, then the short call will hedge the short put up to the value of the premium received from the short call. A similar logic applies if the first leg is a short put.

Second, it will provide additional income if the stock price does fall within the range during the life of the options. Instead of collecting the premium from just selling one option, we get to collect the premiums from selling two options.

Third, it will reduce the margin requirement as compared to that when two unrelated options are sold. If your broker allows you to sell naked options, then most likely he/she will have a lower margin requirement for a short strangle, as compared to the margin requirements for two unrelated short options.

Box 6   Margin requirement for a short strangle

One online broker charges the following margin for a short strangle:-

short naked call : Call Price + Maximum((20% * Underlying Price - Out of the Money Amount), (10% * Underlying Price))
Short naked put: Put Price + Maximum((20% * Underlying Price - Out of the Money Amount), (10% * Strike Price))
Short call and put: If Initial Margin Short Put > Initial Short Call, then
Initial Margin Short Put + Price Short Call
else
If Initial Margin Short Call >= Initial Short Put, then
Initial Margin Short Call + Price Short Put

e.g. current stock price is $50. A call option with strike at $55 is sold at $4.50. A put option with strike price at $35 is sold at $1.50.
Short naked call initial margin: 4.5+max((20%*50-(55-50),(10%*50))=4.5+max(9, 5)=13.5 per share
Short naked put initial margin:1.5+max((20%*50-(50-35),(10%*35))=1.5+max(7, 3.5)=8.5 per share
Initial short call margin > initial short put margin, so
total margin required is 13.5+1.5=$15 per share, much less than (13.5 + 8.5 =) $24

You may ask, why do I suggest selling one option at a strike price that is near the current stock price, and the other option far from the current stock price, instead of choosing strike prices at equal distance from the current stock price. This is because I want to have a very good chance of the options expiring worthless. I am more certain about the range that the stock price will eventually settle within only after it has made extreme moves in one direction: it helps me determine one end of the range. In addition, the volatility of extreme moves will drive up the premium of the options. The drawback is that you will get a much smaller premium on the second option. When the market is relatively calm, on the other hand, choosing a midpoint approach is one of the few ways to earn some income. Either way, we have to be prepared to deal with unfavorable conditions and be able to act fast. Make no mistake, any trade that involves selling options entails high risk.

Box 7   Volatility strategy

When the market was very unstable in August 2011, some practitioners gave suggestions on ways to profit from the volatility. One article that appeared in the Business Times on 17 August 2011 has this suggestion:

"The simplest volatility strategy is combining two types of options to create a range a stock or an index will trade in. This is done by selling a call option, which allows the buyer of that call to purchase shares at a set price, and then buying a put option, which allows the person who owns the shares to force someone else to buy them if they fall to a certain level........The costs would cancel each other out and the investor would have created what is called a collar around the stock."

The article went on to give United Parcel Service as an example, which recently traded at US$63. "..an investor could have sold a call option at US$65 a share for US$2.50 and for the same amount bought a put option at US$60. "
'With volatility kicking up, this is a strategy that more sophisticated investors are taking advantage of," Mr. Vernon (of Biltmore Capital Advisors) said. "They are okay giving up the upside after seeing markets fall down by hundreds of point every day."

Three points to note here. One, it shows that most people are only concerned about downside risk when they talk about volatility. We should remember that volatility is more than that. Options can be used to take advantage of both upside and downside movements.

Second, the article omitted to point out that, for a proper collar set up, an investor should own the underlying stocks in the first place. The addition of the put option serves the purpose of protecting the value of the underlying stocks if the stock price falls, while the selling of the out of money call option is

---

a means to reduce the cost of the protection. The payoff graph of these three positions put together is a reversed Z shape. Taken together, the three positions will have limited profit and limited loss. It is thus not a strategy to take advantage of volatility, but to reduce downside risk.

Third, it would not be adequate to base a decision to set up a trade on the cost involved only. While selling a call option will reduce the cost of the downside protection, investor will have to decide whether the limit on upside gain is worth this cost saving. If we have only the long stock position and put option, if the stock price goes up, as long as the gain in price exceeds the cost of the put option, any excess gain in stock value can be realized.

Example of a short strangle

Let us say that on 16 June 2011, you feel that the price of Google Inc. (GOOG) should be bottoming. You sell a GOOG put option with strike at $430 to expire on 21 January 2012, and the stock price then was $500.37. The premium was $16.763. On the same day, you sell a call option with strike at $750 for $0.684, with the same expiration. The performance of this short strangle from 17 June to 9 December is shown in the graph below:

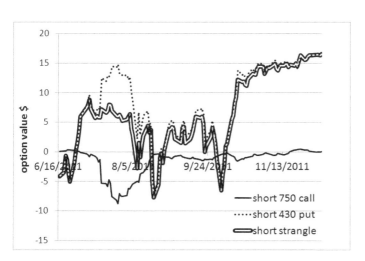

In the above graph, the option value is obtained from subtracting the option premium by the spot option price. For example, we received $16.76 from the short put. When the option price moved to $21.02 on 17 June, the value of the short put was -$4.26. We received $0.68 from the short call option. On 17 June, the short call's price was $0.63. Its value would be $0.05. The short strangle's value is the sum of the values of the two short options, -$4.21.

The maximum profit possible for the short strangle is $16.76+$0.68 = $17.44. If the short strangle's value reaches $17.44, it will be represented by 100% in the graph below. The maximum loss, on the other hand, is theoretically unlimited. During the period shown in the graph, the maximum drawdown was -44.3%.

Performance of Google vs. that of SPY and the short strangle:

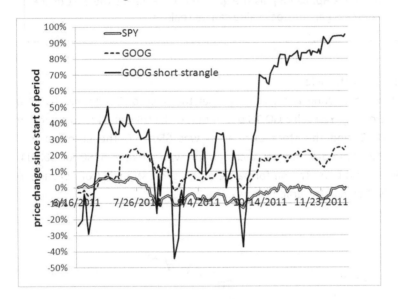

When Google's price shot up on 30 June from $506 to $521 in one day, the two options moved dramatically in opposite direction, and the short strangle's value was dragged down by the short call option. After August, however, the value of the short put option dominated the direction of the short strangle. At first, that was because the price of Google settled down below $550 level, but later, after mid October, even when the stock price went back to near $600 level, the short call value stayed low, demonstrating the accelerating effect of time to expiration on delta: as expiration approaches, delta of OTM option becomes lower.

If we had invested in such a short strangle, and the price of Google Inc. shares continues to stay away from our two strike prices, we could just wait for the contracts to expire in January 2012 and keep the full premiums from the two short option positions.

With hindsight, i.e. with the benefit of the graphs above, however, we could think of ways that investors who are prepared to trade more actively could enhance the returns. For example, our gain from the short call position could be enhanced by replacing it with another short call with a lower strike price when the stock price is relatively high. A more active trader could replace the options even more frequently so that the strike prices hug closely to the peaks and troughs of the stock price as time goes by.

We need to know, however, that more trades do not always mean higher profit. Also, if the stock price jumps outside of our expected range, a short strangle can incur substantial loss because of the leverage built in short option positions. We would have to re-evaluate our bet, and decide on how to adjust the positions quickly.

In sum, a short strangle should be used only by experienced option traders. It can be a good way to profit from option trades with very little capital, provided we take sufficient precautions to limit risk at the start, and are willing to take actions to manage risk after we have entered into option positions.

xiii. Iron Condor

I include Iron Condor simply because of the name given to it. It is a strategy for risk-averse investors that bears a macho name. We saw in the last section that a Short Strangle strategy can yield decent return for you only if you are willing to deal with the high risk entailed. Iron condor aims to reduce the risk of a large increase in the value of either of the two options that were sold by buying further OTM options. The similarity between an iron condor and a reverse iron butterfly is akin to the relationship between a short strangle and a short straddle.

An iron condor is made up of the following option positions:

	Example: current stock price is at $40
Buy 1 OTM Put (lowest)	Long put with strike at $28, premium paid $2.5
Sell 1 OTM Put	Short put with strike at $32, premium received $3
Sell 1 OTM Call	Short call with strike at $48, premium received $3
Buy 1 OTM Call (highest strike)	Long call with strike at $52, premium paid $2.5

Its payoff and profit/loss graphs will look like those shown below:

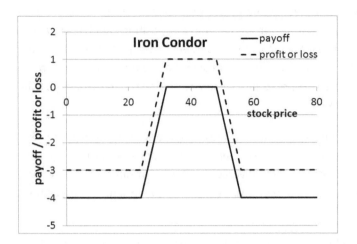

The maximum profit from an iron condor is the net premium received. The maximum loss is the strike price of the long call minus the strike price of the short call minus the net premium received.

The iron condor is a strategy that yields a small profit for a lot of work. If we want to increase the maximum profit, we would need to have a large difference between the strike of the long call and that of the short call, or between that of the long put and the short put. But if we do that, the maximum loss would also increase.

Iron Condor Risk and Reward Summary
Maximum profit is limited to the net premiums received. It occurs when the price of the underlying stock is between the strike prices of the short call and short put positions.
Maximum loss is limited to the difference between the long position and the short position of either the call options or the put options (which should be the same), minus the net premiums received.

Box 8   "Planned return strategy"

How about buying a fund that gives you protection against the first 12 per cent of losses – you will only incur losses after that threshold – and to double the market gains up to a cap of 8 to 12 per cent? This is a fund marketed by a company called MDE Group since 2009. If that sounds good to you, which could well be if the market is as turbulent as it was in August 2011, then here is the even better news: you can run your own "planned return strategy" fund and you do not have to pay management fees. Clue: collars.

xiv. Collars

A collar is made up of the following positions:

A long stock position A short OTM call option A long OTM put option	Example: Buy 100 shares of stock AMZN at $181 per share on 6 Dec 2011 Sell a call option with strike at $190 to expire on 20 Jul 2012 for $21 Buy a put option with strike at $105 with same expiration for $3.35

A collar is basically a covered call option plus a long put. The investor is bearish about the stock's near-future performance. She buys a put option, and then uses the short call to collect some payment to offset the cost of the put option. Or, she could have been using covered calls to generate income on a regular basis, but once in a while feels the need to get protection from extreme downward stock price movements.

Most likely, the investor has owned the stock for a while, and the stock price has gone up decently, so the investor wants to protect the gain with less cost as compared to simply buying a put option. If the investor did not already own the stock, then a bearish opinion could be expressed by a simple put option, or a bear spread, unless the investor's broker does not allow the sale of uncovered calls in the case of a bear call spread, or unsecured put in the case of a bear put spread.

It is possible to set up a collar with net debit in the premiums paid and received, i.e. the premium received from the short call is less than the premium paid for the long put, but this would not make very attractive collars.

Below is a diagram containing the payoff and profit/loss graphs of a collar strategy. The stock was purchased at $43. The strike of the short call is $48, and it earns a premium of $3. The strike of the long put is $32, and the option costs $1 to buy.

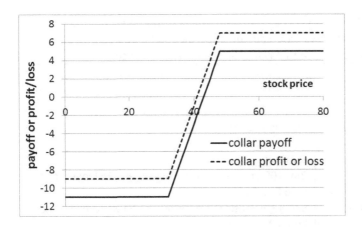

It may seem ironic that the payoff graph of a collar is similar to that of a bull call spread: the former seeks to protect unrealized profit while the latter aims to profit from rising stock price. It is the same with covered call and a short put. The long stock position can make an option position difficult to understand.

If we use the above example in a brochure for a planned return strategy fund, we can say that our strategy provides protection up to the first 5% loss, since the net premium collected is $2, which is 4.6% of the purchase price of the stock of $43. When the stock price goes up to $48, the strike price of the short call, instead of a $5 profit on the stock's long position, the profit is $7, 40% more than otherwise. By looking for the right stocks and juggling with the strike prices (to get higher net premium), we can improve the downside protection as well as upside gain, and thus the attractiveness of our fund. For example, if the net premium that we can get is $3, then the downside protection would be upto the first 7% of loss, and the upside gain would be 60% more than otherwise.

However, our brochure would also have to tell you that if the stock price goes above $48, the gain will not increase any more. The gain from the stock position will be negated by the loss from the short call position (which has a strike price of $48). On the other hand, the loss would not get bigger after the stock price drops to $32 (the strike price of the long put), as any additional loss from the stock position will be offset by the gain from the long put. The maximum loss would thus be $11 (purchase price of the stock minus strike price of put option) minus the net premium received.

Collar spread Risk and Reward Summary
Maximum gain is limited to the difference between the strike price of the

short call option and the purchase price of the long stock, plus the net premium received. It occurs when the stock price equals or exceeds the strike price of the short call option.

Maximum loss is limited to the difference between the purchase price of the stock and the strike price of the long put, minus the net premium received. It occurs when the stock price falls below the strike price of the long put option.

Alternative option strategy

- Dividend capturing with long stock position and short call options

I explained before the relationship between a stock's cash dividend and option price. On or immediately after a stock goes ex-dividend, the stock price usually goes down the same amount as the dividend value, and deep ITM call options will as a result also go down. What implication does this relationship have if you own a call option, the underlying stock of which is going to be ex-dividend in the near future? For example, you just bought a call option with strike price of $70 for $30, while the underlying stock is currently priced at $100. The stock has announced a week ago that it will go ex-dividend three days from now, and the dividend value would be $2. You only learned about this after buying the option.

You have several alternatives.

(i)   Continue to hold the option and ignore the ex-dividend event. On ex-dividend, your option value could go down by $2.

(ii)   Exercise the option now, so that you buy the stock at $70 per share, effectively paying $100 for the stock. When the stock goes ex-dividend, you will receive the dividend of $2 but the stock price will go down by the same amount. You are no better or worse off.

(iii)   Sell the option and buy the stocks. If the option price remains at $30, then this course of action yields the same result as (ii). You get $30 for the option, same as what you paid, and pay $100 for the stock. If, however, the option price is now higher than before, you are better off choosing this over (ii). Alternatively, if the option price has gone down, then (ii) would be better than this alternative.

As shown above, (ii) is a better choice in many instances. This example shows you the potential advantage of exercising an option early.

For institutional investors, or hedge funds, they will also use early exercise to make a riskless option trade. The set-up is like this: they will first buy the underlying stocks just before an ex-dividend date. Then they will sell ITM call options on those stocks. The traders now have covered call positions. The option premium plus the strike price must equal or exceed the current stock price. On ex-dividend, some of option buyers will exercise their options, and a corresponding number of the call options would be assigned to meet these exercise obligations, while the rest will not. The stocks that are not called away because their associated call options were not assigned will be entitled to the stock's cash dividend. They can then sell the stocks after ex-dividend, and at the same time buy back the call options, i.e. close the short call positions. Assuming the stock price drops the same amount as the dividend payment immediately after ex-dividend, and the call option premium also drops the same amount, the option traders can keep the dividend at no risk, because the short option position was fully hedged by the long stock position.

Box 9   "Extreme" options strategies

If we are able to observe certain price patterns in the options market, we can actually devise strategies that could be considered "extreme" in its execution. For example, veteran options trader Jeff Augen detailed in a book how he could employ several different options strategies on the day of options expiration, by taking advantage of the price patterns of expiring options as well as the collapse of volatility on the last hours of an options' life.

One strategy is to profit from the rapidly collapsing volatility by setting up in the last two hours of an options' expiration short straddles with strike price close to the likely closing price of the stock at the end of that day. The price of both options are expected to go down, with the one on the right side of the trade going down more than the options on the wrong side of the trade. While the profit from each short straddle could be small, the risk is also very small.

Summary

We can restate the use of the basic option strategies explained earlier in different ways, such as in terms of:

Options for equity portfolio with core and non-core holdings

You may have an equity portfolio that comprises of a group of stocks that you would like to keep for more than three years (core holding), and other stocks that you intend to trade from time to time to take quick profit (non-core holding). Core holding stocks tend to be large companies in mature stage of growth, while non-core holding stocks could be hot companies for the season or stocks in high growth phase. Instead of being fully invested all the time, and be annoyed by periods of flat stock prices alternated with periods of unpredictable volatility, you could set aside 10 to 15% of the capital for this portfolio for options trading to achieve the following purposes.

(i)   Income generating. Sell OTM call options of stocks in core holding. Our target is for options to become worthless on expiration, so that we can keep all the premiums received.

(ii)   Income generating. Sell ITM or ATM call options of stocks in core holding shortly before dividend distribution, and buy them back (to close the short option positions) once stock price drops after the distribution.

(iii)   Capital protection during market cycles. When stocks in your core holding appear to be overbought, you can buy put options to protect the value of at least some of the core holding stocks.

(iv)   Capital gain from volatile market. Sell ATM or slightly OTM call options of stocks in your non-core holding to take advantage of the high premium during volatile market. You do not mind your underlying non-core stocks being called away (exercised).

The above examples are some of the basic option strategies suitable for a core and non-core holdings portfolio that can be executed with low/medium capital risk and low liquidity risk (all short call options are covered by underlying stock holdings). If done continuously, they could potentially add 3 to 8% to your capital value every year, depending on market conditions and your skills. After you acquire more experience, you could gradually try to use the more aggressive option strategies, such as those that involve naked short option positions to increase profit, but your risk level will increase also.

Options for value stocks portfolio

Value investors buy good stocks when the prices are low, and hold the stocks for a long time, or until the fundamentals become very unfavorable. They are unlikely to sell their stocks even during major market turbulence. They will usually have some cash set aside waiting to buy good stocks when opportunities arise. Using some of that cash for option trading can enhance the value strategy.

Examples of options strategies that are suitable for a value stocks portfolio are:

(i)   Capital gain and stock accumulation during market cycles. When stocks in your holding appear to be oversold, buy deep ITM call options with long expiration such as LEAPS to gain from a gradual recovery of stock price. If the options are still ITM near expiration, you could choose to hold them on expiration so that they are automatically exercised, and you get to buy more stocks at a low price.

(ii)   Income generating. Sell slightly OTM call options of stock holding when the market is relatively calm, or far OTM call options when the market is over exuberant. You basically do not want your options exercised. Your strategy is to have the options expired worthless, so that you can keep the options premiums.

Since value investors are usually long-position biased and have a strong belief in the strength of their stocks, there is no reason for them to buy put options for protection purpose.

Options for a growth stock portfolio

Growth stock investors hold stocks that are in the growth phase, or expected to grow fast in the near future. Growth stock investors should be used to volatility and have no big difficulty in selling a stock when its prospect has changed. If you own a growth stock portfolio, your portfolio can only gain value from stock price appreciation, not from income generation. Option strategies that can be useful for such a stock portfolio are:

(i)   Capital gain on correction: Growth investors know that their stocks can be volatile. A temporary setback in, say, launch date of a new product, can send the stock price down over 10% easily. Buying put options before a potentially bad earnings or product announcement could be profitable.

(ii)   Capital gain on rebound: When their favorite stock is down substantially, growth stock investors may think it is time to buy more. Using simple call options can be a low capital way to gain the same exposure. Using spreads that reduce the cost of call options with short call options at higher strike prices allow one to gain more exposure with the same amount of capital, but the risk also is higher.

The success rate of these two strategies is hard to ascertain. It depends on how well you know your stocks, and some degree of luck. However, if successful, they help to limit the down side and enhance the upside.

Box 10   The real deal about Spreads

When I explained the various types of simple spreads, I made it sound as though their main attraction was in limiting risk while generating a small profit.

The fact is, spreads are popular for one more reason. While short strangles are said to have lower margin requirements than if the short call and short put were sold on different stocks, the formula for calculating margin requirements for simple spreads (i.e. both options are of the same type, either both are calls or both are puts) can be used to drastically reduce the margin requirements of a single short options position.

The margin requirements proposed by the Chicago Board Options Exchange and adopted by many brokers for simple spreads are "the amount by which the long put (short call) aggregate exercise price is below the short put (long call) aggregate exercise price. Long side must be paid for in full. Proceeds from short option sale may be applied", provided the long side expires with or after the short side.

Compare this with the margin requirement of a simple short call position: "100% of option proceeds plus 20% of underlying security value less out-of-the-money amount, if any, to a minimum for calls of option proceeds plus 10% of the underlying security value." (for short put, replace last sentence with:"..a minimum for puts of option proceeds plus 10% of the put's exercise price.")

Say, on 20 January 2013 you want to sell a put options of AAPL at strike of $480 expiring on 16 February 2013, and AAPL closed at $500 the previous trading day. The options price is $14.75. Using CBOE's margins calculator, and applying the proceeds from the sale of the short position, the margin requirement would be $8000.

Now, if you sell the same put options, and at the same time buy a put options with a strike price of $430, and the same expiration, for $3, the total margin requirement becomes $3,825, less than half the margin requirement of the single short put position. So you can set up two pairs of this spread using less than $8,000 margin value and stand to earn 2 times the difference between $14.75 and $3 per share, which amounts to $2,350, and with much less risk than just selling one short put.

The main difference between the two margin requirements is that for a spread, only the difference between the strike prices matters, while for a short put, the margin requirement is dependent on the current stock price as well as the options premium received and the strike price.

6   POSITION ADJUSTMENT

If you had bought a pair of call and put options with the same strike price and expiration for the purpose of profiting from an imminent increase in volatility (in other words, a straddle), and the price of the underlying asset had indeed changed a lot (either up or down) since then, but you worry that it may change direction soon, what should you do?

Position adjustment refers to changes, other than closing the position, to be made to your option position to improve its payoff or prospect. When the stock price movement after you initiated an option trade is unfavorable or may become unfavorable and you feel that it could get worse, you have three choices:

1.   Close the positions by buying back options you sold and/or selling options that you have bought. This will stop any deterioration in the payoff

2.   Add more trades to stop any deterioration in the payoff, and create possibilities for improvement, i.e. undertake position adjustment, or

3.   Do nothing and wait for your option(s) to expire.

You can choose Choice 3 if you hold long positions in options, and that they are near expiration, so that further losses are limited. By letting them expire, you do not have to pay commission for the closing trades, which would be the case if you choose Choice 1.

For example, for the straddle trade, you could lock in the profit by either closing the positions, which means selling the call and put options as in Choice 1, or sell an option of the same type as the one that is currently making money, to lock in some gain from the increased volatility, as option price goes up with volatility. If the stock price has been moving higher, your call option would be making money while the put option is losing money. You should sell a OTM call option (the strike price would be higher than the original options' strike), if you are worried about a change in the direction of the move. This short option will gain if stock price does fall. This is one possibility under Choice 2.

If you have net short positions in executing a strategy, and/or the net delta is high in either positive or negative direction, then adverse stock price movements could cause a lot of damage. As you probably recall, short positions have unlimited downside risk. Even if you have short positions on the opposite sides, e.g. a short call and a short put at different strike prices, the losses in one direction can only be mitigated but not eliminated by gains made by short positions in the other direction. Your better choices would therefore be either Choice 1 or Choice 2.

Sometimes even when there is a lot of time left until your options expire, you could still be forced to decide to take action.

Say you sold put options on Google for $5 per share with strike of $480 when its share price was at $540. Then Google dropped to $490 in a couple of weeks, as in August 2011. Your put option is now asking for $12. You have a paper loss of $7 per share. If you have sufficient funds to meet margin requirement and you truly believe that Google would not fall below $480 on expiration of your option, then you could sit tight and do nothing. However, you could also be taking on too much risk than you know.

If you start to think that Google may have a decent chance of going down a little more when the option expires, or the funds for meeting margin requirements are getting tight, but you still think that Google's price could find bottom soon, then you could adjust your position like this:

First, you exit your current position by buying back the put option for $12.

Then, you sell another put option with strike price at $430, a price that you do not believe Google would fall below before expiration, for $10. While your initial put option has gone up in value, other put options in the series will also have gained value.

On the first trade, you realize a loss of $7. You offset this loss with the $10 that you receive from the second trade. Overall, you maintain a short put option position for the gain of $3. This outcome is of course less desirable than if your original bet was correct, because you would have made $5 instead of $3. However, one thing we must learn in trading options is that it is more important to preserve capital than to prove that we are right.

The shift of the strike price from $480 to $430 will give you a higher chance of making some profit from the trade than if you do nothing. It will also reduce the margin requirement for the trade. If you run out of funds to maintain margin balance, you will be forced to close positions even though the positions could turn out to be profitable if only they could have stayed alive.

Alternatively, you could replace your second trade with selling two put options at even lower strike prices (say $390), if the sum of the premiums of the two options is sufficiently attractive. You figure that, unless most of the properties of the company behind the stock are destroyed by some disaster, there would be virtually no chance for the stock to go down to that level. Thus, even though premium of options that are far out of money is usually small, you could almost be certain that you could keep all of it. You would also be taking advantage of the high volatility of the stock price, which got your first trade in trouble in the first place, because all option prices would be higher than otherwise.

Apart from the probability of keeping the premium, the other difference between the two ways of adjusting the option position is in margin requirement. Even though margin requirement is related to how far a strike price is from the stock price, the margin requirement of two options at lower strike price could still be higher than that for one option at a higher strike price. This would be an important consideration if you are low on funds.

Having a plan to adjust your position before entering a trade, especially ones that involve being in net short positions, is extremely important in option trading.

From the Google example above, you could see that deciding on the adjustments to make on your trade position depends on your diagnosis of the cause of the deteriorating performance. Different causes require different adjustments. Common causes are:

1. Timing. Your direction bet would be correct if only your contract could expire later.
2. Scale. Your direction bet is correct, but the move in option values is not likely to be sufficient to make the trade profitable when all the costs are taken into account.
3. Direction. You guessed one way and the stock price is moving the other way.

4. Option mispricing. Even when you guessed right, the option price moved in a way that is dramatically different from what most popular option model predicts.

If the problem of your trade is resulted from Cause 1, then rolling your option over would be an appropriate adjustment. By this, I mean closing the existing trades and opening similar trades with farther out expiration date and more OTM strike prices. For example, if you had sold a call option of Apple Inc.(AAPL) with strike at $380 to be expiring in one month, and currently AAPL is at $370, and that you believe that the bullish stock sentiment is not going to end too soon, you could buy back the original option to stop it from incurring further losses and sell a new AAPL option that will expire in three months at strike of, say, $420, depending on your assessment of stock price volatility.

When you buy back the original call option, you would probably realize a loss, since the market price of the underlying stock is now nearer to the strike price compared to the price it was probably at when you sold the call option. You would be able to offset the losses at least partially with the premiums collected from the new short call option trade. A variation to this simple roll over is to sell more than one call options at even higher strike price, thus reducing further the possibility of the options becoming ITM and collect more premium at the same time.

Instead of rolling over the short option position, how about not closing the existing position, but add positions to achieve the same objective? You can neutralize somewhat the delta of an existing option by adding something else. For example, you could buy an at-the-money (ATM) put option with the same expiration date, so that any loss from the short put can be covered by the gain from the long put. If the long put option has a longer expiration date, then its delta would be lower than the delta of one with the same expiration date, and the gain from the long position could be less than the loss from the short position. However, the option premium for the long put could be high relative to the premium that you received when you sold the first option, since it is an ATM option. Hence, adding a put option with a longer expiration date would not be a superior adjustment in my view.

There is an unlimited number of ways to adjust your trade position. You can even use the put-call parity formula (see box) to explore alternatives, depending on your risk preference and assessment of the stock price situation. If you wrote a put option, for example, and the stock price has gone down, and looks continue to do so, you would wish that you could change your bet completely. You could buy two put option for each option you wrote, or you could buy a call option and short the stock: this would effectively bring your overall position to neutrality, so that your payoff is not affected by any stock price movement on expiration. Or, if you have a ratio spread, you could enter additional trades to alter the risk profile of the overall position, making it more, or less if you wish, sensitive to stock price movement. If you have a protective put, and your immediate worry has changed from just falling stock price to sudden move in stock price in either up or down direction, you could add an at the money long put to convert the overall position to a synthetic straddle.

What is important is we do the analysis before hand, weighing the costs against the benefits of each alternative and their respective probabilities, so that we can implement the optimal adjustment as soon as circumstances warrant action.

Box 11   Put-call parity

If the cost of borrowing and lending is the same and the call and put option prices have the same implied volatility, then the following formula should be valid, in theory, when no dividend is involved:

$$C - P = S - PV(K)$$

Buying a European call option (C) and selling a European put option (P) at the same time for the same underlying asset with the same strike price (K) and expiration date will give you the same risk and profit profile as directly owning the equivalent number of shares (S) in an option contract, minus a payment that is equivalent to the strike price, K, on option expiration. PV(K) is the present value of a cash amount that is equal to the strike price upon option expiration, assuming a known and continuously compounding interest rate. If this formula does not hold, then somebody will buy the cheaper side and sell the more expensive side and make a riskless profit, the theory goes.

If we plot the payoff graph of a portfolio that contains a call option and a short put option of the same strike, we could see that it is equivalent to that of a long stock position minus the strike price.

Thus, we can synthetically create any equivalent option position using the other components in the formula. To create a trade to neutralize an option position, similarly, we can just add a negative sign to all components in the formula. For example, if we need to neutralize a short put position, we would create

---

111

something that has the same function as a long put position, which is:

$$P = C - S + PV(K)$$

This means that, in theory, we could buy a call option, and then short the same number of shares of the underlying asset as covered by the option, and borrow a cash amount equivalent to the strike price, and then not have to worry about losses from the short put option.

In practice, when you buy a stock at the same strike price as the options in the equation, the stock's profit and loss profile is the same as $S - PV(K)$ in the equation, because you will make profit if the stock price goes above the strike price, and lose money when it goes below the strike price. Hence, $S* = C - P$.

Therefore, for example, you can simulate the effect of holding a call option by buying the stock at strike price and buying a put option. If the stock price goes above the strike price, the put option has no value while the stock would gain. If the stock price goes below the strike price, the long put option will give a positive return, but it will be canceled out by the loss suffered by the long stock position.

What about scale? That is, the direction and timing of your bet is correct, but the size of the option value move is not sufficient to cover costs. You can find ways to add delta in the direction of your bet, as long as you do not increase the cost too much. This would mean a spread, a ratio spread, or writing another option.

If you betted the wrong direction, you should first consider whether it is worthwhile to reverse the direction, which could be expensive, versus simply settling the existing trades (i.e. buying options to close short positions, and selling options already bought). Say you wrote a naked call option at strike of $400, and the current stock price is $395. The option will expire in one month, while the company is set to announce earnings in two weeks. From history, you know that the stock price can be very volatile around earnings announcement time. Moving up or down by over 10% in one day has occurred a few times in the past around such time.

To avoid incurring substantial losses on your naked short call, you could buy an ATM call option, and sell an OTM option to lower the cost, i.e. a bull call spread. If the stock price does shoot up, then gains from the long call option can offset the loss from the naked call, while the OTM short call option will drop a little in value. However, since there is such a short time left, even when there is a ATM call option to offset the loss of the short call, you would still face the danger of the short call being assigned if the stock price shoots up, especially only for one day. When that happens, you would have to deliver the underlying stocks at the strike price, which could be much lower than the market price. In short, you would have to pay the higher market price to buy the stocks and receive a lower price to meet the assignment obligation. Unless you unwind your bull spread at the same time that the naked call was assigned, you would have realized loss on one hand, and uncertain profit on the other. It would seem less risky than to just close the position by buying an offsetting call option.

What if it is a mispricing problem? If there is a lot of time left before your option expires, you could wait and see if the problem corrects itself. If your bet is based on the payoff equation, then on expiration the equation will hold. Else, it would be better to be safe and close the position.

Box 12   BIDU: a day of mispricing?

On 1 February 2012, at 2pm trading time, BIDU's share price was slightly up from the day before's close. It was trading at around $127.7 while it closed at $127.53 the day before. If you had seen the prices of BIDU's options that were to expire on 18 February 2012, you would see that the prices of call options had gone up from the day before, as you would have expected, since higher stock prices would make call options more valuable. However, if you were to look at the prices of BIDU's put options for the same expiration and strike prices at the same time, you would have seen this strange sight: the prices of the put options were also higher than those of the day before. For at the money strike of $130, for instance, the option price went up from $6.51 to $7.50. For out of money strikes of, say, $110, the price increased from $0.69 to $1.08. I have the screenshot from my broker to prove the existence of these prices, but I do not have permission to publish it.

How can the prices of put options go up when the stock price goes up? Was it because volatility had gone up? Volatility did not go up on the day concerned, nor the day before. Also, for put options expiring in March 2012, their prices behaved as expected: they went down, but so did the prices of call options for March! There is no obvious explanation to this strange price behavior of BIDU options. One possible explanation is the effect of an announcement made on the early hours of the day that BIDU's quarterly earnings report would be available on 16 February. This date was earlier than what was rumored, but later than the usual announcement of Q4 results in end January.

This to and fro in earnings announcement date might have created mayhem

---

among option traders, since the month in which the earnings would be announced had switched from January to before expiration of March contracts, then back to February. It may have suddenly increased demand for both put and call options that were going to expire on 18 February, two days after the scheduled earnings announcement. Those who owned Baidu shares, for example, might want to buy put options for protection purpose, while those who were optimistic about Baidu's earnings might want to profit from a surge in stock price when the earnings were announced. They therefore switched from the March options to the February options.

More digging would be required to verify the validity of this theory, but it certainly sounds plausible to me. The pricing models of options do not always capture all the factors at work, and thus 'mispricing' can occur from time to time.

How should investors view such 'mispricings'? I would think that in the long term the prices will become 'correct' again, and in the mean time, investors can try to find trading opportunities from such events. For example, could the rush to buy February options create an overbought situation? If so, we could try to profit from it by selling the options!

Actually, the 'mispricing' situation described above happens more often than we think. One situation that this happens is when price of a stock changes direction in a short time. This is one example to remind us that we should not over rely on theoretical formulae in predicting option price directions. There are more factors at play in real life than what have been captured in most pricing models.

7 THE ROLE OF OPTION TRADING IN PORTFOLIO MANAGEMENT

Traditionally, portfolio managers would regard options as a type of derivatives that belongs to the basket of alternative investments. I would argue that we can choose to use options as part of our equity portfolio by selecting particular option strategies.

Box 13	A story about strategies

Just like stock investing or in life, there are many different ways to win. Which one works for us depends on whether the strategy harnesses our strengths and avoids our weaknesses. The best illustration of the importance of choosing the right strategy is an ancient Chinese story. In the Tang Dynasty, there were two lords who both loved horses. They both claimed to own the fastest horses in the country. Many races were held, and their horses were always neck to neck. One day, the two lords decided to have a final match to decide on who could actually claim to have the fastest horses. There were to be three races, and the winner of at least two races could claim the title.

Lord Chen lined up the three races with his fastest horse in the first race, second fastest second race, and the third fastest horse the last. Lord Tsui chose a different strategy. He put his third fastest horse in the first race, the fastest in the second race, and the second fastest horse in the last race. No price for guessing who won.

What is the role of options in portfolio management if we regard them as an integral part of our equity portfolio (as a subportfolio in the whole portfolio of investable assets)?

Portfolio management refers to the approach of managing a person's investable assets as a whole package, instead of looking at them individually. Different types of assets, such as stocks, bonds, real estates, precious metals and so on are said to have distinct risk and reward profiles as well as behave differently under the same economic circumstances. Using their differences to alter the overall risk and reward profile of the whole portfolio is the essence of portfolio management.

The most famous theory in portfolio management is the Modern Portfolio Theory developed by Harry Markowitz. Markowitz said that if you plot the standard deviation of the returns of each asset (as a measure of risk) against the return of the asset on a graph, and do the same for all the possible combinations of such assets, each pair of asset returns and its standard deviation being represented by a dot on the graph, these dots will, taken together, look like an upward sloping curve (referred as the Efficient Frontier). The curve below illustrates that there is often a trade-off between risk and reward. To get higher returns, one often has to take higher risk. It also shows that, by owning two assets instead of one, it is possible to increase expected returns without increasing risk, or reduce risk without a drop in returns. The key to achieving this incredible feat is to find assets that perform differently from each other over time, that is, assets that have low correlation.

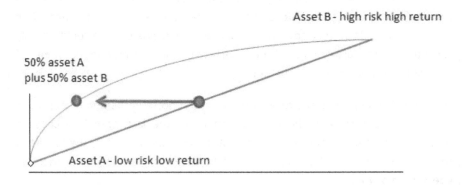

The above diagram contains two points that represent the risk and return of two different assets, Asset A and Asset B. The vertical axis is the expected return of an asset (or assets), while the horizontal axis is the standard deviation of the return. There is a straight line and a curve joining the two points. The straight line represents the risk and return of all possible combinations of the two assets, if we disregard the effect of correlation between the two assets, or if the two assets' price movements do not have any correlation. For example, if, whenever the price of Asset A moves, the price of Asset B does not, and vice versa, then the two assets are said to have zero correlation.

Let us also assume that Asset A and Asset B have the same return-to-risk ratio, that is, if we divide the expected return of Asset A by the standard deviation of the price of Asset A, we will get a value that is equal to the expected return of Asset A divided by the standard deviation of the price of Asset B. This means that the straight line joining the two points will go through the (0,0) coordinate of the graph, and that the performance of Asset B is like that of a bigger investment in Asset A.

The curve connecting the two points is the joint risk and return of all possible combinations of the two assets if the two assets' price movements are negatively correlated, i.e. when the price of one goes up, the other one would go down. For a particular combination of the two assets, such as 50/50, we can see from the arrow on the graph that the risk level on the curve is lower while the return is the same, as indicated by the value on the vertical axis of the two small circles.

How does option trading fit into portfolio management? Traditionally, options are grouped with other derivatives and are considered an asset type that is different from equities. I prefer to regard stock options as part of the equity portfolio. If our souped-up equity portfolio can have a lower correlation with another asset than that of a plain vanilla equity portfolio, and the combined return is at least no worse than the combined return of the plain vanilla equity portfolio and the other asset, it would support our case that stock options can enhance overall portfolio performance if treated as part of the equity subportfolio.

Obviously, there are so many option strategies and each has its unique risk return characteristics that it is not possible to lump them together and say, this is the combined performance of an equity portfolio that includes stock options. To demonstrate the possible role of stock options in portfolio management by becoming part of the equity subportfolio, we have picked two option trading strategies: protective put and covered call. We will apply the two strategies on the stock index fund, SPY, which is an exchange traded fund that aims to replicate the performance of the S&P500 index. Options of SPY are settled by physical delivery of the shares. Description of the two strategies is contained in the box below.

Box 14 Test models
Assume that we start this equity portfolio with $100,000 of cash at the start of a period. In either strategy, we will use the cash to buy as many shares as possible

---

immediately after the start of the period. On 3 January 2006, SPY opened at $125.19 per share, i.e. 789 shares could be bought, leaving $98.38 in cash.

Protective Put for SPY
Whenever SPY price falls by 3% or more in 10 <u>trading</u> days, we will use 1% worth of portfolio value (sell shares if cash is not enough) and buy as many puts as can be afforded (but not to hedge more than the number of shares held) at a strike price at least 5% below the current SPY price, adjusted for number of days to expire (based on a 30 day month). The put options should expire in the current month if there are more than 14 <u>calendar</u> days to go, or the next near month. The purpose is to protect the portfolio partially against sharp fall in SPY price in the near term.

The put options will be held to expiration.

Once a batch of options is bought because of the fall in SPY, we will use 1% of portfolio value (excluding market value of active options) to buy another batch of options only when SPY price drops more than 3% for two consecutive 10 trading day periods. We will also buy another batch of options if SPY price has dropped more than 3% for each of three consecutive 10 day periods, provided no more than one batch of options are bought on the same day. At any one time, there will be no more than three batches of active options.

Whenever the cash balance exceeds the price of a share, it will be used to purchase the maximum number of shares on the next day.

Covered Call for SPY
The 789 shares bought can be used to cover 7 call options contracts. We will sell the maximum number of call options as can be covered by the shares owned at the start of the period and on a monthly basis at a strike price that is at 105% of the spot price (to be adjusted on a 30 day basis, i.e. if an option is to expire in 50 days, the strike price would be higher than if it were to expire in 14 days). The options will expire in the current month unless there is less than 14 calendar days left, in which case we will sell options to expire in the next month.

If an option is exercised, we will buy back the shares in a short period of time (within ten days), first at 99% of the exercise price, then, if unsuccessful, at spot price, so that we do not have to worry too much about missing out on gains if the market goes up.

If an option's strike price is less than the spot price of SPY at any time before option expiration, we will assume that the option will be exercised if the time value is less than 2% of the value of the strike price. This assumption could be a source of error, because option buyers may decide to exercise at higher or lower threshold. The outcome of this difference cannot be predicted.

When shares are bought back, call options will be sold on the next day for the near month that has at least fourteen (14) calendar days to expire, else the premium could be too low to cover expenses.

Our target with this strategy is to add about 2% extra gain to the portfolio value on an annual basis, as compared to buying and holding SPY.

We calculated the correlation of the performances of these two strategies with that of a bond index fund called Vanguard Total Return Bond Market ETF(symbol is BND), which is an exchange traded fund that attempts to track the performance of the Barclays Capital U.S. Aggregate Float Adjusted Index, an index that measures the returns of a broad group of investment grade fixed income securities in the USA. Because BND was launched in mid 2007, the correlation calculation used monthly data of the bond index fund and the souped-up equity portfolios from January 2008 to December 2011. We modified the data of BND to include reinvestment return to simulate the performance of BND as if dividends were ploughed back to purchase shares.

This is the result of our backtesting:

	Correlation with BND
SPY buy and hold	0.166
SPY with protective put	0.080
SPY with covered call	0.219

A correlation of 1 means that the two assets are perfectly correlated: when one goes up, the other does also. A correlation of -1 means that the two assets have perfectly negative correlation: when one goes one way, the other goes the opposite direction. An asset has correlation of 1 with itself. All three equity portfolios shown in the above table have a positive correlation with BND, but the correlation is quite low. It means that, if a investor of BND decides to switch some of her holdings into any of the three equity portfolios, she will have a chance of getting higher (or lower) returns without much increase in overall volatility (a measure of risk level). Of the three equity portfolio, SPY with protective put offers the lower correlation, and thus the possibility of lower increase in volatility, than the SPY buy and hold portfolio.

While lower volatility is regarded as a plus by many investors, all investors are concerned about the returns. The combined return of two or more assets is the weighted average returns of the assets. Combining an asset with other assets will only improve the risk return profile if, in exchange for slightly higher volatility, it will not reduce the overall returns. Let us now find out which of the three equity portfolios can give the best result if combined with BND, if past performance is repeated.

	Total Returns 2008-2011
SPY buy and hold	-14.15%
SPY buy and hold with reinvestment	-7.02%
SPY with protective puts	0.07%
SPY with covered calls	0.17%
BND	25.62%
BND with reinvestment	46.08%

The three equity portfolios did worse than BND in the four year period. To save time, I have not included the reinvestment of dividends in the two equity-with-options portfolios, but the results are unlikely to be different: they gave better returns than the SPY buy and hold portfolios, and the SPY with protective put options had lower correlation with BND than the SPY buy and hold portfolio. It would therefore seem likely that either of the equity-with-options portfolio would be a better partner for BND in achieving higher return with a smaller increase in volatility.

Performance among the equity portfolios
Because of the global financial crisis in 2008, bonds did much better than stocks in 2008. To compare the three equity portfolios over a longer period of time, I calculated the returns of the three portfolios over a six year period, from 2006 to 2011.

	SPY buy and hold (no	Protective put	covered call

	reinvestment)		
2011	-0.20%	2.27%	6.32%
2010	12.83%	8.04%	16.15%
2009	23.46%	15.46%	37.05%
2008	-38.25%	-15.47%	-31.10%
2007	3.24%	0.78%	4.10%
2006	13.11%	9.14%	13.97%
overall	0.24%	18.63%	38.34%

While inclusion of reinvestment of dividends might improve the performance of SPY buy and hold, I doubt it would be sufficient to change the conclusion, that both covered call and protective put strategy would improve the performance of the equity portfolio *during the period analyzed*. I have not backtested the strategies for sufficiently long periods of time to be able to say that they would work in all circumstances. From the above results, we can say that, it is likely that the protective put strategy would work very well during times of great distress in reducing the scale of drawdown, while the covered call strategy is likely to improve the performance of an equity portfolio slightly in normal circumstances and a bit more during time of high volatility, resulting in a significant gain over several periods of time.

8   CONCLUSION

This book has provided hopefully an easy to understand explanation of the basic characteristics of options, how they are traded, major factors that affect option prices, and the common option strategies. I hope I have convinced some of you to see options as useful companion to your stock investing. You have seen how options can help us take advantage of situations that pure stock trading cannot make use of, and how they can be used to protect our equity positions if we do so sparingly. Once we recognize and accept their characteristics, which can be dramatic and seemingly unruly at times, options can be used fruitfully and safely.

Not only are there many ways to use options, you can also choose (with a lot of care) to use options that match your investment psychology and habit, such as how often you would like to trade, how closely can you afford to monitor the position, as well as your level of risk tolerance. Notice how I spent more time on the four very basic option strategies, because once you understand how those work, you can figure out quite a bit about how complex strategies work.

The book also gave two examples of how equity holdings could be used together with options to improve the risk-adjusted performance of the whole portfolio in the context of portfolio management. We saw how the same options strategy would work better in certain market/stock condition, and only so-so under other conditions. This is a reminder that we should not expect an option strategy to work in a similar way under all circumstances.

The evidence that more and more stock investors find it necessary to use options to enhance the returns from stocks is growing. Just take a look at an article (excerpted in table below) that appeared in Yahoo Finance in February 2012. In one breath, it covered recommendations for three strategies to profit from the circumstances faced by investors at that time. (Having read this book, you should now have no trouble in naming the strategies mentioned in it. But can you also spot an error?) This is a good development for people who know how to trade options, as higher liquidity will reduce cost for everyone. It also means that stock trading on its own is seen as unlikely to produce adequate return compared to the risks involved in the foreseeable future. Options trading is set to become a necessary part of stock trading in our life time.

Box 15   Media article suggests the use of options
Source: http://finance.yahoo.com/news/markets-greece-deal-wheres-big-192128562.html

Markets Get Greece Deal, So Where's the Big Rally?   CNBC, 10 Feb 2012
"......The dynamic of waiting for Greece to resolve and anticipating when and if the Fed will roll out a third round of asset purchases known as quantitative easing sets up an investor dilemma. The central bank last week said it will keep lending rates near zero and hinted that QE3 was on the horizon.

Some in the market already are preparing for another round of uncertainty by implementing more stringent safety strategies.

"Unless the situation in Europe unwinds in a way that's not one of the scenarios already in the market - and the market has quite a few scenarios discounted - being heavily diversified with a barbell strategy has helped clients," says Quincy Krosby, chief market strategist at Prudential Annuities in Newark, N.J.

The strategy involves concentrating in annuities and defensive stocks like staples, utilities and health care - which, notably, have performed poorest this year - and a lesser allocation toward riskier strategies like options.......

As for options, using them indeed involves substantial risk and isn't for the inexperienced.
But with the market's main gauge of fear, the CBOE Volatility Index (INDEX: VIX) around its lowest level in seven months, downside protection is fairly cheap.

"You can buy puts cheaply, you can buy calls cheaply," Rick Bensignor, chief market strategist at Merlin Securities in New York, says of options that respectively allow holders to sell or buy stocks at a certain level. "That's a strategy to look at if you think the market has a chance of not sitting here. Volatility is cheap enough that options may be a better way to play than stocks."

Options volume has been on an uptick in the early stages of 2012, averaging about 17 million contracts a day, according to the Options Clearing Corp. Volume had slowed in November and December but was near 19 million contracts a day in October.

In this climate, traders would be smart to sell calls on high-quality companies whose stock you also own, says Brian Stutland, head of Stutland Volatility Group in Chicago. The strategy provides income from selling the put contract, which gives the holder the option of buying a stock at a specified price and date, while also allowing for appreciation of the stock.

"You can lower the breakeven," he said, referring to price point at the stock where the owner would make a profit. "You're almost creating a synthetic dividend payment for yourself."

Another strategy for those not looking for big market moves is selling calls that are slightly out of the money - or below the current price - to increase chances of a payoff in a market that doesn't change much.

Michael Cohn, chief market strategist at Global Arena Investment Management, employs a twist on the approach - he's actually buying slightly out-of-the-money calls on an exchange-traded fund that pays when the stock market falls.

The premium for the calls is relatively inexpensive and it allows Cohn exposure should the rally exhaust itself and the market move lower...."

INDEX

CPSIA information can be obtained at www.ICGtesting.com
Printed in the USA
LVOW01s1201080215

426171LV00049B/1719/P